Giovani Felipe Jahn
Vinicius C Garcia

Architecture for Handling Unstructured Data

Giovani Felipe Jahn
Vinicius C Garcia

Architecture for Handling Unstructured Data

A Proposed Architecture for Handling Unstructured Data at Federal Education Institutes

ScienciaScripts

Imprint

Any brand names and product names mentioned in this book are subject to trademark, brand or patent protection and are trademarks or registered trademarks of their respective holders. The use of brand names, product names, common names, trade names, product descriptions etc. even without a particular marking in this work is in no way to be construed to mean that such names may be regarded as unrestricted in respect of trademark and brand protection legislation and could thus be used by anyone.

Cover image: www.ingimage.com

This book is a translation from the original published under ISBN 978-613-9-61515-5.

Publisher:
Sciencia Scripts
is a trademark of
Dodo Books Indian Ocean Ltd. and OmniScriptum S.R.L publishing group

120 High Road, East Finchley, London, N2 9ED, United Kingdom
Str. Armeneasca 28/1, office 1, Chisinau MD-2012, Republic of Moldova, Europe
Printed at: see last page
ISBN: 978-620-7-73630-0

Content index:

Chapter 1   4

Chapter 2   17

Chapter 3   47

Chapter 4   53

Chapter 5   66

GIOVANI FELIPE JAHN

VINICIUS CARDOSO GARCIA

2

ARCHITECTURE FOR DATA PROCESSING NO STRUCTURED

SUMMARY

One of the trends to solve the various problems and challenges generated by the context of *Big Data* is the movement called *NoSQL (Not only SQL)*, which promotes several innovative solutions for storing and processing large volumes of data. The works available in the literature related to *NoSQL* explain, in addition to its emergence, systems available for manipulating data that require efficient, scalable and broad processing power. Which also drives the creation of *NoSQL* data processing systems it is your inference to complex data, semi-structured or unstructured , present today in social networks, sensors, Internet *logs , among others.* In view of the challenges regarding data manipulation and processing in this context, a new set of tool platforms focused on *Big Data* has been proposed, many of them in the form of *open source* or free licenses , proving to be excellent vehicles for developing solutions. for processing data of this nature. This work aims to present a reference architecture for processing unstructured data , so that it can provide analysis on data from local networks, social networks, intranets, the internet and any connected device. Initially, the work exposes the concepts, languages and tools of the main technologies regarding *NoSQL* . Products such as Hadoop, Hive, HBase denote the large number of *NoSQL* solutions available on the market. Next, a survey of institutional data shows that the processing of unstructured data is still considered a first for these institutions. A theoretical-conceptual methodological approach was used , adding paradigms from the DSR (*Design Science Research*) method to give the research solid and potentially relevant knowledge when developing a proposal for a reference architecture for processing unstructured data within the scope of federal education institutes. The creation of an adequate conceptual and technological framework for *open source* tools encouraged this proposal.

Chapter 1

1. INTRODUCTION

This chapter presents the motivations, framework and justifications for carrying out this work. The general and specific objectives , the methodological approach and its steps, which guide the research, are also described, followed by the literature review strategy . Finally, the structure of the work is presented.

1.1 Problem

unstructured data from diverse sources such as social networks, *web* content , local networks, IoT devices, among others, is imminent. This data is useful to organizations from the most diverse segments, including Federal Institutes of Education. Based on this premise, a primary question arises: how to best treat this data, aiming to benefit from what a Federal Institute of Education proposes ?

1.2 Motivation and Framework

The data produced by networks linked to the Internet reaches its users in the most diverse formats and in increasingly larger volumes, humanly immeasurable. The processing of this data, for analytical purposes, as well as the complexity of this type of work only increases and where to store it is an equally frequent concern . The best way to have access to this data, without it just being a clutter of space and time, are projects involving *Big Data in the Cloud* environment . The use of hybrid clouds by Institutions Federal Education, Science and Technology has been a reality for some time. It then becomes convenient to add to these new trends in the processing of unstructured data , originating from various devices interconnected to networks, the Internet, IoT, social networks, among others.

In general, this data can be mined [1]to provide valuable *insights* and knowledge for educational institutions , which means that using *Big Data* meets the mission of these institutions. Data mining adds veracity to the visualization of student performance , for example, promoting recommendations and actions by teachers. Likewise, analytical methods can suggest everything from how to treat certain student behaviors to recommending courses or educational activities aimed at specific content. Furthermore, according to Wassanr (2015), educational institutions are using analytical data to improve the services

---

[1] Data mining is the process of discovering actionable information in large data sets. Source Microsoft.com.

provided, given the growth of students and courses. The use of *Big Data platforms* and programming models , such as *MapReduce* , can accelerate the analysis of educational data. And, much more than just capturing data, it is up to the institution within this reality to transform it into useful information for its educational management , as well as adapt its actions.

Within the *Big Data* phenomenon , *Open Data* sources , especially with regard to government data, incorporate benefits such as transparency, social control and participation. Such benefits, according to Giffinger et al . (2007) are inherent to *Smart Governance* (transparency), *Smart People* (participation in public life) and *Smart Economy* (entrepreneurship). According to this premise, one can assert that *open data* provides encouragement for the issues in question, in educational institutions . It should also be noted that, as it is a public body that is an effective part of a government, the use of *open data* complies with the Access to Information Law (Law No. 12,527, of November 18, 2011). The government's use of open government data improves the organizational efficiency of public sectors, the creation of new products and services, as well as social benefits (MANYKA et al . , 2013).

use of Information and Communication Technologies (ICT) is recommended as a way of qualifying services provided in the areas of education. Inherent to this, it is important to know which database technologies are available, how they work and what benefits they could bring in an educational context , regarding data processing, so that future choices can be made about these when implementing applications to be used by federal educational institutions . To this end, an exploratory analysis of these technologies is appropriate and very useful.

Rewarding the aforementioned arguments, associated with a context involving unstructured data , this study also aims to show that certain information, if collected and analyzed, can serve as support for the individual 's learning and training processes , in addition to encouraging the promotion of research.

1.3 Goals

1.3.1 General

Propose a reference architecture for processing unstructured data .

1.3.2 Specifics

a) Present the state of the art in *Big Data, Analytics , NoSQL themes* ;
b) *NoSQL* databases ;
c) Compare the ways of processing data;
d) Identify the techniques and tools used for unstructured data processing solutions ;

e) unstructured data (*NoSQL*), identified with the reality of the Federal Institute of Education, Science and Technology Farroupilha; It is

f) Build knowledge within the scope of the Federal Institutes of Education from the study of unstructured data .

In this way, it is initially expected to characterize *Big Data* and *NoSQL Data* , as well as the role of the latter in relation to the former. Secondly, carry out a study and analysis of tools and methods that can compose an architecture, aimed at the reality of Federal Institutes of Education, in particular IFFar (Federal Institute of Education , Science and Technology Farroupilha), for the processing of unstructured data .

1.4 Methodological Approach

methodological approach guiding this work is theoretical - conceptual based on a literature review (exploratory). The objective, according to Vergara (2005), is to explore an area that presents a lack of systematized knowledge. Considering that the area that encompasses *NoSQL* technologies has not yet produced a vast or complete collection on the subject, it is pertinent to explore more intrinsically the term itself, bibliographies, products offered on the market, among others, with the aim of carrying out an analysis regarding the advantages that can be obtained in contrast with the reality of IFFar. The DSR model is used to corroborate the effectiveness of the research.

The adoption of methodology here means choosing a certain path taken in stages, under certain rules, but not obstructing creativity, helping the author to think critically, have discipline, develop and write this work, with due regard for methodological and academic standards . It identifies how mental operations are processed in the scientific research process and systematizes it into distinct steps, showing the procedures adopted in each of them.

1.4.1 Characterization of the research

Research is a rational and systematic procedure that aims to seek answers to previously proposed problems (GIL, 2002). Still based on this author, this work is considered as technological research, as it is concerned with producing a functional construct . Regarding the procedures adopted, the research is entitled bibliographic-exploratory (GIL, 2002), as it uses countless bibliographic sources, articles, periodicals, books, theses and other research.

It is worth highlighting, according to Cervo and Bervian (2002), that research is an activity aimed at solving theoretical or practical problems using scientific processes when there is a problem and there is no information to solve it.

Despite this, Daft and Lewin (1990) justify the need for modernization in terms of research methods , as well as their suitability for the problem investigated. It suggests that organizations adopt Design *Science* methods , as these would be the predominant vehicles for meeting the rigorous requirements of research. Romme (2003), from the same perspective, emphasizes that studies involving organizations require greater dedication and states that such studies must include Design Science in their research, as this is the most concise form of knowledge production . However, in order to operationalize these concepts, ensuring due rigor to the research, it is necessary to adopt a method compatible and inherent to the one proposed. This research method is called *Design Science Research* (DSR).

Combining a theoretical-conceptual methodological approach based on a broad literature review , together with Design Science and, therefore, guided by DSR, contributes to the success of the research. Based on this paradigm, this is the proposal adopted to build a construct-type artifact, allowing work inherent to the organizational environment of IFFar.

1.4.2 Bibliographic-exploratory research

The purpose of this research is defined as exploratory, which characterizes it as having greater familiarity on the part of the researcher with the topic, and can be based on hypotheses or intuitions. It suggests a larger bibliographic survey , in which citations and examples aim to facilitate understanding of the matter. In the opinion of Babbie (1986), exploratory research , where it is possible to control effects that distort the researcher's perception , allows reality to be perceived as it is, and not as the researcher thinks it is.

As for the means, in turn, the research is conditioned to be bibliographic, as for the theoretical and methodological foundation it was necessary to investigate the following subjects: *NoSQL* , *Big Data* , data architectures, tools for data processing, among others related subjects and terms. Investigations characterized in this way are widely used in exploratory research and rely heavily on the researcher's intuition .

To make the theories transcribed in the previous paragraphs factual , academic search engines such as *Web Science* [2], IEEE [3], *Scopus* [4], *Google Scholar* [5], *Digital Library were used* [6], in addition to other vehicles that brought promotion and elucidation to subjects relevant to the topic of this research.

1.4.2.1 Literature Review Strategy

[2] webofknowledge.com
[3] https://www.ieee.org
[4] https://www.scopus.com
[5] scholar.google.com.br
[6] http://dl.acm.org

The literature review aims to acquire knowledge to absorb the updated context in which the unstructured data related to the proposed objectives and related to the problem previously presented are inserted.

The literature review is one of the main pillars of this book. In addition to understanding the current state of terms inherent to research, a conceptual approach to the available tools and architectures is necessary . The review was initially designed to be carried out gradually, starting with the most generic terms and later more intrinsic and specific ones, such as architectures related to *NoSQL , open source* and freely licensed tools for *Big Data and processing of* unstructured data , in addition to insertions pertinent to the ramifications of issues within different scenarios and circumstances .

Therefore, the relevant terms are inserted in academic and scientific repositories , such as: " *Google Scholar", "Scopus", "Web Of Science", "IEEE"* and *"ACM Digital Library* ", taking into account the year of publication of the articles, their relevance according to their number of citations, in addition to associations between authors in the area. The key concepts used in the research were those contained in Table 1, giving priority to the period 2013-2017, obviously not abandoning productions of content deemed significant to the research context, which were outside this chronology.

bibliographic review process , the searches took place on more than one platform, with numerous documents initially were found, containing the presupposed terms. Subsequently, a brief viewing of most of these was necessary , to then filter the content and consequent acquisition of the material.

Table 1: List of terms searched in repositories and quantity returned in number of articles/dissertations/theses

	Google Scholar	Scopus	WebOf Science	IEEE	ACM Digital Library
Big data	12,300	387	235	281	158
NoSQL	15,900	1,331	810	602	182
NoSQL Database	7,920	1,201	623	538	80
NoSQL Clusters	71	122	83	74	1
NoSQL Engine	57	135	56	65	two
NoSQL Architecture	65	272	159	147	1
NoSQL Education	1	24	9	9	0
Hadoop	+ 28,300	4,964	3,183	2,961	510
MapReduce	+ 16,600	5,105	3,575	3,123	657

				282	0
BigData Architectures	0	0	0	282	0
BigData Analytics	322	78	53	61	11

Source: Prepared by the author (2017)

From that point onwards, refinements were implemented in the research, so that the practices of reading abstracts, full articles , material cited in these and other sources could be more objectively resumed .

Among the documents read, those that were most significantly associated with the initial proposal of this research work, or that produced relevant subsidies , are measured in Appendix A.

1.4.3 DSR

When studying artificial phenomena , which, unlike natural ones (describe the interactions and behaviors of nature), are those created by humanity, an attempt is made to satisfy needs, desires and objectives (VAISHNAVI and KUECHLER, 2009). These authors argue that *Design Science* is an appropriate method for studying phenomena of this origin, as it has techniques for constructing artifacts that satisfy its assumptions, using design, analysis, reflection and abstraction.

Vakkari (1994) adds, stating that information science is synonymous with applied science , and, therefore, a "project class", therefore, *Design Science* is a science that develops technological artifacts to meet the practical needs of organizations, institutions or individuals.

The main mission of *Design Science* is to develop knowledge for the design and development of artifacts (VAN AKEN, 2004), therefore it is correct to state that *Design Science Research* (DSR) is a meta-theory that allows the researcher to create artifacts through processes, processes that by In turn, they create knowledge, thus justifying the scientific nature of the research. Therefore, when producing an artifact, scientific knowledge is generated to improve or perfect the processes inherent to an organization or institution.

Van Aken (2004) brings us a quote that very opportunistically expresses the core of what is proposed as a methodology based on DSR: "A *Design Science* it is not concerned with the action itself, but with the knowledge that can be used to design solutions" (VAN AKEN, 2004, p. 228). According to Hevner et al . (2004), DSR seeks to identify and address real problems in a real world, proposing practical and appropriate solutions to solve them, through the construction and application of an artifact. These artifacts can be constructs, models, methods or instances of a system, constructed and evaluated from the perspective of the problem it is intended to address.

Lacerda (2013) is a little more emphatic when he suggests that DSR is a core method for technological research proposals , effectively resulting in rigorous scientific production , when well conducted.

The DSR process begins when the researcher becomes aware of the "problem", which is the initial condition for starting the research. Identifying the problem and its context is essential for understanding and delimiting the studied environment, and

Starting from this context, motivate and justify the importance of the research to be carried out. This awareness can come from multiple sources, and results in a formal proposal for a new research effort (VAISHNAVI and KUECHLER, 2009).

The next phase is " suggestion", where the researcher, based on the problem, defines the objectives to be achieved by its solution. Once the objectives are listed and, based on the state of the art in your area, this creative stage begins in which propositions are suggested that may encompass a reconfiguration of existing or new elements (VAISHNAVI and KUECHLER, 2009).

Based on the suggestions, the "development" stage begins, which effectively deals with the construction of the artifact to solve the problem. This development must comply with DSR metrics regarding the construction of an artifact.

For DSR, an artifact is the organization of the components of an internal environment, as a means of achieving success in achieving objectives in a given external environment (SIMON, 1996). Once the artifacts have been defined, they can be typified . Artifacts can be defined as: Constructs, Models, Methods and Instantiations (MARCH; SMITH, 1995).

It is important to emphasize that, when it comes to developing a solution, we are not invariably, or exclusively, focusing on product development. DSR perfectly meets this purpose, however, it has broader objectives: generating knowledge that is applicable and useful for solving problems, improvements to something that already exists or even the creation of new solutions (artifacts) (VENABLE, 2006) .

" Evaluation", the final stage of DSR, is defined as the rigorous process of verifying the behavior of the artifact in the environment for which it was designed, in relation to the solutions it was intended to achieve.

In view of these arguments, it is possible to summarize that DSR allows a research problem to be resolved, without disregarding the scientific rigor necessary when producing new knowledge, nor disregarding the applicability of this solution in a real situation . This time, these concepts meet the proposal of this research on the processing of unstructured data in a specific institutional scope .

Regarding the work proposed here, it is suggested to arrive at a technically based artifact to solve the problem of processing unstructured data at the institutional level . The research steps are systematized in Figure 1.

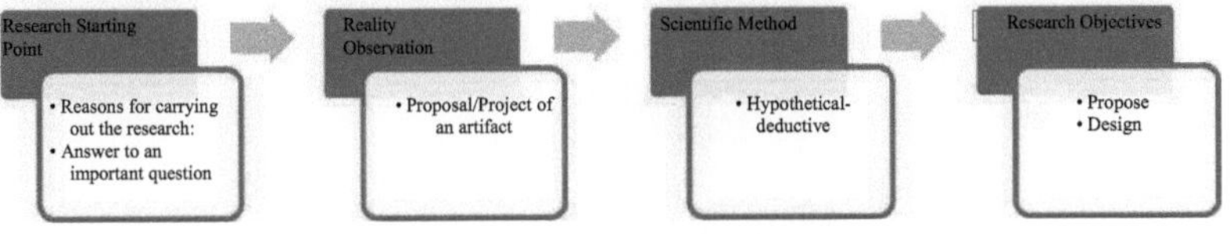

Source: Prepared by the author (2017)

1.4.4 Phases of the methodological approach

Once the definition of the problem has been explained, the research will begin . According to Marconi and Lakatos (1990), in the scientific area, a problem refers to any unresolved circumstance that is an instrument of discussion, in any area of knowledge, thus arousing the researcher's interest. The objective of the proposed study is then the solution to this problem. However, it is essential to initially check whether the suggested problem qualifies as "scientific". Furthermore, according to Marconi and Lakatos (1990), a problem, whether practical or intellectual, is scientific in nature when it involves variables that can be tested, observed, manipulated through methodologies. This research proposal fits the requirements imposed.

After defining or identifying the problem and with outlined objectives, Dresch (2013) recommends becoming aware of its repercussions for the organization.

The results that this research seeks to achieve are then outlined by the proposition of general and specific objectives, and point to a more exploratory and explanatory nature, without, however, depriving themselves of the descriptive.

A work plan is then drawn up to effectively guide the steps and tasks inherent to the research. From this, a systematic review of the literature is carried out, seeking to establish a table containing the solutions available to date.

1.4.4.1 Construction of a Work Plan

According to Marconi and Lakatos (2010), the work plan constitutes the chain of logical steps, adopted by the researcher, with a view to achieving success in his objective, as well as generating truly recognized knowledge. Carrying out a broad and careful exploratory review of the literature aims to objectively find techniques that can be used to design the reference architecture for processing unstructured data . Of equal seriousness, conceiving concepts about areas, tools and applications on large-volume unstructured data becomes essential and primary attitude for the success of said proposal. The concepts presented in Figure 2 are highlighted:

Figure 2: Work plan

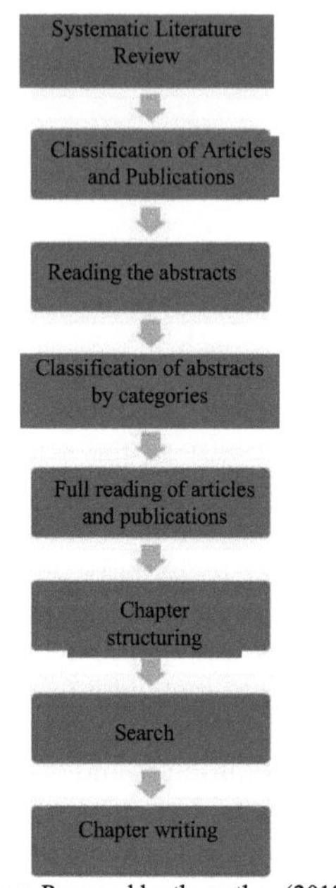

Source: Prepared by the author (2017)

1.4.4.2 Data Collection

To continue the research , data collection was necessary , subdivided into two spheres. One in literary repositories , with the purpose of providing technical and theoretical resources, summarized by Figure 3:

Figure 3: Summary of data collection in literary repositories

Source: Prepared by the author (2017)

Another data collection was carried out at the educational institution , through research aimed at employees, which served to bring to light the reality of IFFar, with regard to the level of knowledge on the part of IT analysts and technicians on the topic " unstructured data ." It was applied as a *survey* , to anchor the research objectives. The diagram in Figure 4 summarizes the work carried out regarding these inferences.

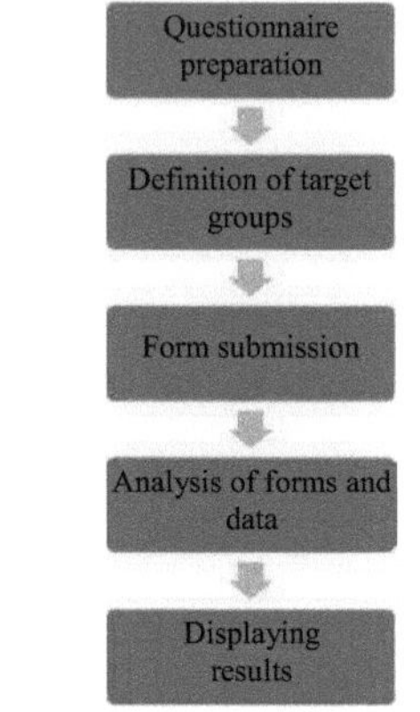

Source: Prepared by the author (2017)

1.4.4.3. Solution Proposition

With the techniques found in the review, supported by the concepts and forms of data processing and also the institutional situation , it is possible to propose a reference architecture to meet the requirements and quality attributes regarding the processing of unstructured data .

1.4.4.4 Assessment

The evaluation of a research proposition is certainly one of the most striking characteristics of scientific activity ; it can be, and most of the time is, applied at all stages. However, it concerns that at the end of the process, a more careful evaluation must be imposed on the final product, one that seeks to respond to the problem and that contemplates, or not, the objectives proposed by the researcher. Such assessment will address general, methodological and ethical issues and will be based on concise and reliable methods .

In order to fully achieve, or attempt to achieve, these evaluative paradigms, this work submits, to specialists, the proposed architecture so that, through their review, through a descriptive method , it is evaluated, accepted, refuted or analyzed and commented on.

In this way and according to Hevner et al . (2004), the form of evaluation used is descriptive, as it uses relevant research on the subject to corroborate the arguments that highlight the usefulness of the construct. Such evaluation seeks to demonstrate the usefulness of the developed artifact.

Furthermore, it should be noted that this proposal is a reference architecture only. Reference architectures are generic and aim to meet *stakeholder* [11] considerations regarding a specific domain. In *this* prospectus, there is no specific method for evaluating this type of architecture, unlike what we could find in software architecture evaluations . specific.

---

[11] Term used in several areas , such as project or software management , among many others, referring to interested parties.

1.4.4.5 Data Collection About the Evaluation of the Proposed Solution

In order for a high level of incontestability of the assessment to be achieved, some steps were taken to prevent the method, which is shown in Figure 5:

Figure 5: Steps in the evaluation process

Source: Prepared by the author (2017)

Therefore, the methodological approach during this work suggests:
a) Define the research question "How can an architecture for processing unstructured data be useful to federal educational institutes and, therefore, IFFar?";
b) Propose objectives to be achieved;
c) Build a work plan, describing steps;
d) Carry out the work and writing of this book, with technological composition ; It is
e) Comply with the research methodology through a literature review guided by DSR, as support for this work.

1.5 Structure of the Work

This book is divided into six chapters.
The initial chapter provides the reader with a brief introduction to the reasons and motives that led to the emergence of this research, as well as the strategy for research used

for the literature review and the proposed objectives. The chapter describes the methodological approach to the research, in addition to a contextualization of the DSR method . At the end of the chapter, the structure of the document is presented.

In chapter two, dedicated to the theoretical framework and conceptual framework, the literature review is elaborated . Firstly, the aspect of *Big Data* is addressed , dissecting its adjacencies so that the reader takes possession of knowledge on this topic, whose definitions also fit into the context of unstructured data , given the close relationship between the two terms. There is also a technical overview of *NoSQL* databases and data processing tools.

Chapter three shows the details of the research to arrive at an architecture proposal for processing unstructured data in the environment of federal education institutes and the presentation of a reference architecture proposal , based on *open source* and free solutions . license.

Chapter four presents the reference architecture that the author considers relevant to the research objectives, aimed at use by Federal Institutes of Education.

The fifth chapter aims to evaluate the proposed architecture, presenting the development of the architecture through proposed scenarios, which take advantage of unstructured data , storage and distributed processing , highlighting technologies such as Apache Hadoop [12], HBase [13], HDFS [14], Kafka [15], Tableau [16], among others.

In the last chapter there are conclusions and future propositions. It presents the conclusions of this work and raises possibilities for future work.

---

[12] http://hadoop.apache.org/
[13] https://hbase.apache.org
[14] https://hadoop.apache.org/docs/r1.2.1/hdfs_design.html
[15] https://kafka.apache.org/
[16] https://www.tableau.com/

Chapter 2
2 THEORETICAL FRAMEWORK

With the purpose of presenting some fundamental concepts about the themes covered by this research, this chapter proposes to introduce the main concepts that guide it. Among them, the characteristics of *Big Data* , *Analytics* , *NoSQL* , *among others,* are necessarily included, so that, through a more detailed conceptualization , more concise approaches to data processing can be made , with a timely emphasis on unstructured data . , in addition to the existing aspects around models and tools.

It is first worth remembering that the relational database model was (and still is) present in many data processing systems. However, the growth in the intense volume of data in organizations, associated with the anxiety to obtain useful information for the market or management , has led to the emergence of alternative models to the relational one, also driven by a need for scalability of these systems. These models are currently called *NoSQL* , and their scope has been growing and gaining strength, both in academic and commercial environments.

NoSQL systems They are not "tied" to tabular structures, presenting greater flexibility and not being dependent on schemas.

With the significant increase in the number of users connected to social media and the Internet as a whole, IoT devices and many other segments that generate diverse data, it is essential that there is a means capable of storing and carrying out a reliable and agile analysis of this data .

It is important to emphasize that concepts of adopting *NoSQL* technologies are present in Big *Data* domains (VIEIRA *et. al.,* 2012). Talking about unstructured data falls into improving *Big Data paradigms* . Therefore, it is worth starting this reference with a dissection of this topic, identifying tools inherent to its treatment and then adding, to this context, specificities of *NoSQL* .

2.1 *big data*

The premise of accelerated growth on an almost immeasurable scale of data generated by the computerized society is what defines the term *Big Data* . Supported by technological changes , the once fictitious aspect of a scale in the zettabytes is now an adjective for even domestic use . As an example , White (2012) brings to light the previous statement by measuring and citing some companies such as Facebook [17], which stores more than ten billion photos, comprising more than a petabyte of stored information .

In addition to the accelerated scale at which increasingly larger volumes of data are created, *Big Data* is characterized by the heterogeneity and quantity of connected devices and users and the fact that the use of information and communication technologies are used for the most everyday routines. performed by a user (MAYER-SCHÖNBERGER; CUKIER, 2013). Not only are people responsible for producing data, electronic equipment of the most diverse categories and characteristics has also become a major generator of data records.

Big Data emerges rooted in the purpose of extracting data that exceeds the

---

[17] network founded in 2004 by Mark Zuckerberg, Eduardo Saverin, Andrew McCollum, Dustin Moskovitz and Chris Hughes, students at Harvard University.

conventional processing capacity of database systems, transforming them into useful, inherent and pertinent information at the same time they are processed. Such data, in addition to being excessively large, moves quickly through media and does not fit into restricted conventional database architectures. For these reasons, it is mandatory to use specific tools capable of processing large volumes, so that any and all information in these media can be found, analyzed and used in a timely manner (FAN and BIFET, 2012).

> *Big Data is a new term used to identify datasets that we can not manage with current methodologies or Data Mining software tools due to their large size and complexity.* (FAN and BIFET, 2012).

Briefly, Kim, Trimi and Ji-Hyoung (2014) define the term *Big Data* as an enormous amount of digital data, collected from countless sources. Marth and Scharkow (2013) complete the above statement by adding that these data sets are too large to be handled by regular storage and processing infrastructures.

Delving a little deeper into the term *Big Data* within the literary segments, we see, and it is necessary to add to this, other important characteristics in addition to the already measured expressive volume. The origin of different sources of this data is consistent with variety, as well as the real time in which this data is processed to generate information reduces speed (MANYIKA et al . , 2011; MCAFEE & BRYNJOLFSSON, 2012).

The variety of data sources is directly related to the most diverse systems, applications, tools, equipment, connections and users involved in capturing the data, most of which are currently in an unstructured form . Yes, they are images, audio and video *streams* , texts, Internet logs, among many others (DAVENPORT, 2014) .

Of equal relevance to the previous aspects, there is the characteristic of speed. In short, the data generated is available in real time, simultaneously and immediately for its creation, analysis and processing, supporting instant decision- making (MCAFFE; BRYNJOLFSSON, 2012).

The aspect of exaggerated volume is imminent here. Petabytes of data are generated every day, and it is estimated that this number will double in a few months. It is also variety, since, as already mentioned, this data comes from structured and unstructured systems (the vast majority), generated by emails, social media (Facebook, Twitter, YouTube and others), electronic documents, presentations, messages instant cameras, sensors, RFID [18](*Radio-Frequency IDentification*) tags, video cameras , and much more. Speed, because we often need to act practically in real time on this immense volume of data.
In addition to these three "Vs", it is perfectly plausible to add two others to the concept of *Big Data : veracity and value (DEMCHENKO et al . , 2013).* According to the author, the reliability of the data needs to be proven in terms of its origin and authenticity, in addition to this data must make sense. As for value, Demchenko (2013) implies that this means working with data that actually makes sense and that are sources of added value for decision-making , a basic principle for the return on investments in *Big Data projects .*

2.1.1 *Big Data* Paradigms

It is stated that the technologies, still current for the majority, but effectively from the past, with regard to data processing are no longer adequate. What factors support such a prerogative? It is worth contextualizing the so-called *Big Data* paradigms here , with the main purpose of solving this unknown assumption and highlighting the properties that new systems for data processing must possess .

---

[18] Radio frequency identification

already been mentioned several times in this compendium that the enormous amounts of data on the Internet have created the need for technology that allows companies , institutions, bodies to extract value from this random data and in different formats, in an efficient, agile and that results in information that generates knowledge or profitability. *big data* is this technology.

Regarding large volume data, it is necessary to be able to handle the entire wide variety that characterizes them, defined as follows in terms of data types: Structured - data that has well-defined formats, such as that extracted from spreadsheets or relational databases in the SQL format [19]; Semi-structured – Similar to structured data, but not completely obedient in terms of form. In this line are the records of languages based on HTML and XML; Unstructured or *NoSQL* - does not have a specific format, it is data collected in its original form, such as text, a video, an email fragment, a system log or even a mere photo.

When Edgar F. Codd [20], in 1969, proposed the relational model for databases [21], the demand was solely for data with a defined structure, of internal origin in the companies that proposed to use it. Such a model, obviously, was not designed to handle unstructured data , for the simple fact that this was unimaginable at the time, nor for volumes on the order of terabytes/petabytes/exabytes/zettabytes, seen in contemporary times. Therefore, the model created by Codd was fully satisfactory, as well as simple, for the chronological context in which it found itself.

It bears repeating that the need for new models to process data on the scale of volume, variety and speed of *Big Data and the emergence of NoSQL* database systems materializes.

The aspect that involves analyzing the data captured is also a preponderant factor when we mention *Big Data* . In the conception of Davenport (2007), *Analytics components*[22] They are extremely important when it comes to converting data into business value, coexisting with the traditional *Business Intelligence* [23] systems that exist today.

Furthermore, according to Marz and Warren (2015), complexity, scalability, robustness and ease are the main properties that define a *Big Data system. A formal* review of these properties is in order here :

a)   Fault tolerance : the very concept of distributed [24] systems , in itself , makes this characteristic somewhat difficult to achieve. However, it is plausible and necessary to make systems behave robustly, despite the randomness of the nodes that make up the *clusters* , complex semantics , data duplicity, competition and other situations inherent to distributed systems. This context suggests that, for *Big Data systems* to have robustness and fault tolerance , the shortest path is to avoid unnecessary complexities , focusing on the reason for the existence of this system, which it proposes. This makes the incidence of human errors more difficult, in addition to making it robust.

b) *Big Data* system Scalable is what has the ability to process data in increasing volumes, without losing performance and without failing to satisfy growing demands in the same proportion. In short, it is the ability to maintain system performance when data

---

[19] *Structured Query Language*

[20] Edgar (Ted) Codd, IBM mathematician , known for creating the "relational" model for representing data.

[21] IBM, 2016 https://www-03.ibm.com/ibm/history/exhibits/builders/builders_codd.html

[22] A data - centric approach that combines the science of predictive analytics with advanced business intelligence capabilities .

[23] BI - a technique to assist managers in strategic planning

[24] distributed system is a set of independent computers that presents itself to its users as a single , coherent system " – Tanenbaum and Van Steen (2008)

or load increases, and when *hardware* and *software resources are reduced.* are requested from the system. The Lambda [21] Architecture , with its horizontally scalable feature , becomes an ideal example to explain this property, as it adds more machines to the set of *clusters* when greater performance is needed.

c) Low latency: Latency requirements for reading and updating vary greatly from one system to another. However, for *Big Data systems* , it is essential to be able to work with low latency, especially when it comes to updates, without compromising robustness.

d) Extensibility: Changes, whether planned or not, in *Big Data* systems cannot compromise any of the qualities that this system brings. An extensible system allows the developer to add a new feature or change, without compromising possible data migrations or incurring high costs to do so. Making a system extensible means facilitating migration processes , on a small or large scale, quickly and easily .

e) Agile debugging and minimal maintenance: even when a system is already considered stable and robust, this does not mean that errors in the future or throughout its existence are unlikely. It would be considered utopian to predict perfection throughout the entire existential process of a system. In *Big Data systems* , the aforementioned predictions serve and, in this way, they must offer conditions

favorable conditions and transparency of information regarding the need for debugging when something goes wrong. Traceability of data values is also essential, to identify possible erroneous actions that the system may commit. Equally important is the maintenance of that system. Maintenance are actions previously stipulated by the developer of a system. In *Big Data,* this involves anticipating when to add machines to *clusters* , keeping processes running and debugging anything that has gone wrong. A maintenance -minimizing factor is to choose components that have the lowest possible implementation complexity. The more complex a system, the more likely something will go wrong. The complexity of a *Big Data system* is combatted by the use of simple algorithms with simple components.

2.1.2 Classification of *Big Data* According to its Categories

Big Data can also be characterized a little more , through a synthetic classification into categories, with the purpose of bringing the reader a little more detail about how data is treated and the processes involved, in addition to formalizing some standards for this. :

a) Regarding the type of data analysis - real-time analysis ; subsequent analysis (by batches of data);

b) Regarding the processing method - it comprises the technique applied in data processing. It can be *ad hoc* , analytical, predictive or reporting. It is also pertinent to combine more than one of these techniques, chosen according to the purpose and purpose of the system;

c) Regarding data types – means the classification of data types to be processed according to the system's classification directives , such as transactional, historical, implicit, explicit and others;

d) Regarding the format of the data - in terms of form, the data can be structured (relational databases), semi-structured (XML files) or unstructured (images, audio, video, text, logs);

e) Regarding the size and frequency of the data - it comprises the estimated volume and how often this data undergoes processing. Determining these two requirements in advance helps to define how the storage will be carried out, in terms of the mechanism used, format and the tools necessary for processing to be as optimized as possible. The sources that determine frequency and size are: on demand, social media data , for example; real-time *feed , which* is transactional (weather) data , for example; time series , which are data based on time intervals;

f) Regarding the source of the data – they understand the origin of the data source, whether it was generated by any device, a connected computer generating logs, web pages , social networks, among others. Identifying all data sources helps determine the scope of a perspective on the objectives of the *Big Data system* (BI, business, behavioral analysis);

g) Regarding data consumers - a list of all possible consumers of the processed data is listed:

- processes ;
- corporate users ;
- enterprise applications
- individual people in various business functions ;
- part of the process flows;
- other data repositories or enterprise applications.

h) Regarding *Hardware* – the entire *Big Data* solution It will be based on a type of physical equipment (*Hardware*), which will be responsible for "running" the system. Choosing *Hardware* it is directly proportional to the performance of the Big *Data* solution .

2.1.3 Importance of *Big Data*

massive growth in the use of *smartphones* , sensors and other data-producing devices, associated with the use of cloud computing and improvements to the Web, as a routine for individuals and institutions, clearly exemplifies the technological advances experienced today. Such advances contribute to a greater volume, speed and variety of data produced. This is a fact that generates countless examples of the importance, both of *Big Data sources* and of the concept itself, inherent to computational systems for decision-making, as shown in the following transcripts.

The Google Trends [25]service corroborates in proving that the term *Big Data* is as important as its effective benefit. In recent years, demand on the subject has grown exponentially, as well as *hardware* and *software computing tools and devices have emerged* to quickly process and apply data of large volume and variety.

More than just a gigantic pile of data, *Big Data* represents the promotion of the production of information of a structured and unstructured nature , giving it the characteristic of a generator of data about data, metainformation about individuals and users, with influence directly and indirectly on these. Inherent in all professions, Big *Data* influences the relationship between the use of the powers that knowledge produces. The use

---

[25] https://trends.google.com.br/

of this technology associated with *Machine Learning algorithms makes it possible* [26]to highlight user trend scenarios , assume administrative decisions, infer government decisions in certain areas, actions unimaginable without using an approach based on these paradigms. This makes clear the concept that the term *Big Data* It is not only related to large-scale collection and storage , but obviously also involves processing this data to add value to the context in which it is applied.

These prerogatives suggest applicability preferably in *Business Intelligence systems* , however, they mean equidistance of applicability in educational environments or institutions .

The relationship between data, information and knowledge is indisputable , in the sense that the first two aggregate the third (CHOO, 2006). The main purpose of collecting adequate information is to be useful, from a strategic and functional point of view , to organizations. Furthermore, knowledge has been increasingly recognized as the most valuable asset in institutions. Therefore, for organizations to be successful they must be able to capture, integrate, create and use knowledge in a disciplined, systemic and strategic way (SAMBAMURTHY; SUBRAMANI, 2005).

It is equally correct to say that a significant amount of data is produced daily about each user, reflecting our commercial, political, social, personal and private activities. We leave digital traces about what we like to eat, places to visit, declared loves, dislikes and generalities.

The use of social networks, purchases, various registrations, transactions, among many other activities carried out through the Internet, generate a significantly large amount of data about each subject. Companies, government agencies , various entities, are increasingly able to obtain information relating to the individual, such as location, personal preferences , affinities and even sentimental phase, in a precise and insightful way. In this sense, the potential control that *Big Data* can assess in terms of strategic, social, political and business control becomes obvious .

It can be considered that we are currently living in the era of data explosion , where the amount of data created and stored has an almost immeasurable volume (ZIKOPOULOS et al . , 2012). Despite being a relatively new term, *big data* is present and growing in all sectors of society. Companies like Google or Netflix make use of a constant stream of complex data for millions of requests in real time. Another example is business companies , which take advantage of the immensity of data provided by users on social networks, considered useful for discerning their taste and preferences in relation to a product or service offered, with the clear objective of strengthening the relationship between supplier and consumer.

It should be noted that the data needs to be of quality, so that it becomes meaningful for use, producing benefits for institutions. According to Salvador et al. (2006), data has quality if it meets the following precepts:

> - Accurate: it is the measure of how correct, how free of errors, how close this data is to the true fact. It is a fundamental measure of data quality; if one piece of data is not correct, the other dimensions are less important. To be correct, a value must be certain and must be represented in a consistent and unambiguous way.
> - Available on time: the data is sufficiently updated for the tasks that require it;
> - Relevant: important to the decision maker in a context; is useful and applicable

---

[26]Type of Artificial Intelligence that facilitates a computer's ability to learn and essentially teach itself to evolve as it is exposed to new and constantly changing data . Source: http://computerworld.com.br

to the task at hand;
- Governance and Data Quality according to DMBOK
- Complete: it must contain all the important facts, in the breadth and depth appropriate to your needs;
- Simple/Understood: avoiding the so-called " information overload";
- Reliable: depends on the source or collection method . (SALVADOR et al., 2006).

scenario, a great challenge arises imminently regarding the subject of *Big Data* : how to filter, understand and use the data generated? Overcoming this challenge requires first gaining access to this extensive set of non- homogeneous data, generated and propagated on an immeasurable scale. Likewise, another challenge, also an opportunity, is the fact that managers have the ability to use this large volume of varied unstructured data from countless sources , such as smartphones, social networks, blogs, among many others (DI MARTINO et al. , 2014) in decision-making processes, as institutions are dealing with an expansion of data that is incompatible with traditional management and analysis methods , which leads to the need to think of new ways to do so, in order to generate pertinent information and timely (DAVENPORT, 2012).

Regarding government bodies - educational institutions are characterized as such - it is worth highlighting here some preambles about open *data* .

It is pertinent in the sense that the educational institution can use consultations of different natures to compose useful information available to society.

It is common to find an association between *open data* and *open government* , however, in addition to conceptualizing both, it is necessary to emphasize that they are not synonymous. While the reference to the term open data *is* relevant to data that can be freely used, reused and redistributed by anyone, as long as they are subject to source attribution and sharing rules (OPEN DATA HANDBOOK, 2014) and do not restrict its use and sharing by third parties, regardless of the purpose. The term open government *translates* into a set of initiatives that seek to give the State greater transparency and responsibility, in addition to, according to Barros et al. (2010), propose technical, semantic and organizational standardization in the production and dissemination of data and public information, which would indirectly imply greater responsibility for the State in terms of resource management and improvement in the provision of public services.

Describing data as "open" implies some requirements: allowing redistribution, reuse , availability - preferably on the Internet - and modifiable access . There can also be no discrimination regarding any area of activity, as well as groups or individuals - an educational-only title, for example, no longer characterizes the data as open (OPEN DATA HANDBOOK, 2014).

In line with the assumptions mentioned about open data, it can be stated that, for the existence of an open government characteristic , it must necessarily make use of *open data concepts* . Making government data available, under the title of open, aims to break down existing barriers between citizens who use public service information and the State. For convenience, citizens must be guaranteed access to, as well as understanding, public data, according to their interests.

In this way, the primary idea associated with *Open Government Data*[27] is to make available and allow sharing of the largest possible amount of official "government" data.

---

[27] https://opengovernmentdata.org/

From these premises emerges the "jargon" e-gov (Electronic Government), understood as one of the main forms of modernization of the State. A new paradigm of digital inclusion , which has the citizen as its main subject, while allowing the State to offer public services with higher quality, reduce costs, simplify processes, improve management and be transparent (CHAHIN et al . , 2004).

According to Matheus, Vaz and Ribeiro (2014), Brazil has been evolving towards becoming an open government. Initially using only static pages with financial reports , moving on to the adoption of transparency portals and finally, *datasets* [28]in an open format (Open Government Data - DGA). However, even though there is progress in this aspect, it is important to highlight that simply making information available on government portals does not ensure the necessary transparency. According to Paiva and Revoredo (2016), in a related article, the large volume of data and non-standardization are the causes that still make this practice and the effective systematic monitoring of this data unfeasible. They also report:

> The solution to this type of problem is through the application of data processing techniques that allow the structuring of information in a clearer and more enlightening way for the population. To achieve this, it is necessary to develop tools capable of processing this large volume of data and allowing a consolidated visualization of this information [...] (PAIVA, REVOREDO, 2016)

On the other hand, there is only meaning in having open data if the citizen expresses initiative, or at least curiosity, in reusing it according to their interest. However, there are still obstacles to this. The majority of information from public authorities is still presented in forms that are proprietary or incompatible with all individuals (people with disabilities), devices and

equipment. Therefore, it is necessary to impose that institutions prone to publishing government data do so according to some principles:

a) select which data will be made available;
b) identify and hold data controllers accountable;
c) present this data in a reusable and user-friendly format; It is
d) publish and disseminate the data.

In addition to these, according to OPEN GOV DATA (2007), the data must be characterized by:

a) complete - All public data is available, without privacy, security or access control limitations ;
b) primary - Presented as collected at the source, without modifications;
c) current - Made available as soon as created, to preserve their value;
d) accessible - Widest possible reach of users and for the widest possible set of purposes;
e) compatible with *Hardware* - The data must enable automated processing;
f) non- discriminatory - Available to everyone, natively;
g) non-proprietary – Available in any format, without system, application or software exclusivity; It is
h) license -free - The data is not subject to any copyright, patent, intellectual property or industrial secret restrictions .

Still related to the topic just mentioned, it is pertinent to talk about data governance (GD). Data governance is understood as the set of practices, processes, standards, technologies and policies of accessibility, availability, quality, consistency and security regarding an organization 's data (PANIAN, 2010), used as a tool for creating data

---

[28]Tabulated dataset

guidelines. control of this data.

Institutions , from the most diverse areas, can take different paths regarding how to act on data governance . There are, for example, methodologies
different models for the same GD paradigms, such as Data [29]Governance programs from Oracle , IBM [30], and DMBOK - *Data Management Body of Knowledge* (DAMA, 2015). However, regardless of the main focus that the institution directs, some objectives are considered common in any type of data processing policy by governance. They are , according to Fernandes and Abreu (2012):

a) allow better decision-making;
b) protect the needs of *stakeholders* ;
c) institutionalize common management in handling data problems;
d) build standards, processes and methodologies that can be disseminated throughout the organization;
e) reduce costs and increase effectiveness by coordinating joint efforts ; It is
f) ensure the transparency of processes.

Finally, it is worth highlighting that IFFar, a public institution with its own governance , does not abstain from the responsibilities and inferences, directly or indirectly, imposed by the precepts of data governance . It is up to it, when proposing to govern through the processing and/or analysis of data, to strictly comply with the requirements imposed by these concepts, previously mentioned.

2.1.3 *Big Data* Analytics

Big Data Analytics is translated , didactically, as an analysis of large amounts of data. And in fact that is what it is. It consists of using advanced analysis tools on a significantly large volume of data, with the aim of providing intelligent information , through the use of extremely high- performance software.

It brings together a set of actions that involve searching for data, subsequently processing it and with the aim of generating *insights* for decision making strategies, through in- depth analysis . All of this was carried out in the shortest predictable period of time , as defined by Russom (2016).

> [..] User organizations are implementing specific forms of analytics, what is sometimes called advanced analytics . This is a collection of related techniques and types of tools, typically including predictive analytics , data mining , complex statistical analysis , and SQL. We can also extend the list to cover data visualization , artificial intelligence , natural language processing, and database capabilities that support analytics (such as *MapReduce* , database analysis , in -memory databases, columnar data storage) . Instead of "advanced analytics", a better term would be " discovery analytics" because that 's what users are trying to accomplish. In other words, with big data analysis , the user is typically a business analyst who is trying to discover new business facts that no one in the company knew before. To do this, the analyst needs large volumes of detailed data. (RUSSOM, 2016)

The main objective of *Big Data Analytics* can be translated into: optimizing work processes, acquiring valuable *insights into market* trends , consumer behavior, identifying the profile of a certain audience and forecasts.

---

[29] http://www.devmedia.com.br/governanca-de-dados-implementando-a-gestao-e-governanca-de-dados/30915
[30] https://www-01.ibm.com/software/br/data/info/information-governance/dm.html

To be successful in terms of its stated purposes, Big *Data* analysis software *seeks* support from the following sources:

a) social media content ;
b) statistics from IoT-connected sensors;
c) surveys ;
d) email texts;
e) log files;
f) data from *Business Intelligence tools* ;
g) business reports ; It is
h) economic indicators .

There are billions of active users on social networks who share millions of information, photos, videos, *tweets* [31]in a day and who are connected, presuppose data for the collection, storage and analysis of *Big Data Analytics tools* , for example through *Big Social Data* [32]. Such information allows corporations, institutions and governments to draw more specific and segmented profiles on these users, making decision-making more relevant to their purposes.

2.1.4 *Big Social Data*

Online social networks , at present, are gigantic repositories of personal information , interactions between users and between institutions, opinions on subjects of an almost infinite nature, identifiers of trend scenarios and much more. In view of this environment, the importance of analyzing social networks for various segments, including educational entities, emerges clearly and clearly. It is therefore appropriate here, in connection with the purpose of this research, to explain some topics inherent to social networks and the benefits of their analysis.

According to Wasserman (1994), a social network is defined by the existence of relationships between a set of actors (users/profiles). Furthermore, França et al. (2014), in a timely article, compares a social network to a living organism, giving a synonym for user, to its cells . It suggests that users of a social network (like an organism) may have a long lifespan within the network, while others will be there momentarily, with a short and defined purpose . Content disseminated in this cited article also reveals to us that the participants, grouped together by the characteristics and/or objectives of an individual in a social network, tend to relate to the peers of another individual, forming a close connection between these we call us, conceiving then a "web" of users of immeasurable magnitude .

The author also opportunely emphasizes:

> The tendency for people to come together and form groups is a characteristic of any society [Castells, 2000]. This behavior is portrayed, nowadays, through the advancement of social media and online communities that highlight the power of uniting users around the world. Content generated by its users has reached a high degree of reach through their comments, reports of events almost in real time, experiences, opinions, criticisms and recommendations that are read, shared and
>
> discussed, almost instantly, on various platforms available on the Web. (FRANÇA et al.,2014)

Therefore, the great amount of information from these users provides abundant

---

[31]Name used to designate publications made on the *Twitter* social network .
[32] http://www.inf.ufpr.br/sbbd-sbsc2014/sbbd/proceedings/artigos/pdfs/127.pdf

material for analysis, with the aim of filtering information, which will serve as a subsidy for a multitude of actions, such as: advertising and *marketing* tactics , analysis of market trends , political formation , promotion of events, dissemination of research, entertainment, combating harm - terrorism, among many others.

In view of this, it is correct to induce the reasoning of how important the analysis of data from *online social networks* can be , which, given its magnitude in volume and variety, adds to it the adjective *Big Social Data* , or *Big Data* in networks social. This volume of content produced and shared on *online social networks* , by the large number of geographically dispersed users , is a source of new and continuous information, which can be added to existing information from different areas. This challenge of analyzing this wide variety of data must be viewed from the perspective of the available tools for processing unstructured data .

Identifying the relevance of social media data analysis , as well as its correlation with educational entities and despite this, the way in which this data could be collected, analyzed and used effectively to produce various subsidies for institutional management , will also do, even which indirectly forms part of this research statement.

2.1.5 The Context of Using Big *Data* and *Cloud Computing*

It is already a reality that cloud computing environments are being used to manage data in the form of *Big Data* . Cloud technologies associated with *Big Data Analytics concepts* tend to offer a low-cost distribution model for data analysis , through Databases as a Service (DaaS) [33] and Infrastructure as a Service (IaaS) [34]. According to Lome (2009), infrastructure provided as services provides elasticity, backup automatic and agility in implementation at costs specific to the necessary demand . On the other hand, DaaS is capable of providing remote management of servers located in an external infrastructure, and at reduced costs.

Likewise, it is important to mention that, as cloud computing grows, companies providing cloud services intensify the provision of services and consumers of these services improve the construction of more agile and efficient environments to take advantage of this offer. It is prudent to take the management of IT organizations to actions that look at cloud computing as the framework to support the processing of unstructured data . Environments of this nature require *clusters* of servers that support tools for processing large and varied volumes of data. Inherent to the fact, clouds are made up of sets of servers, which allows for both an increase and decrease in the resources offered to the user, depending on their real need. Ultimately, it is an economical way to provide support for *Big Data* and more advanced analysis technologies. These aforementioned resources, and many others, are no longer under the responsibility of whoever will use them, but are being replaced by third-party platforms with the purpose of allowing the use of on-demand services , regardless of physical or geographic location , associating a high degree transparency and costs appropriate to use.

Brantner et al . (2008) defines cloud computing as *Utility Computing* , an evolution of IT services , whose main objective is to provide storage, processing and bandwidth[35]

---

[33] *Database as a Service* (DaaS)

[34] *Infrastructure as a Service* (IaaS)

[35]transmission capacity of a given medium, connection or network, determining the speed at which data passes through this specific network .

scalable, in the form of goods for consumption, through specific providers , at a cost equivalent to the user 's claim . *Backups* , infrastructure availability, read and write access are transparent to the user. The provider is solely responsible for making the data available in a timely manner, through server replicating methods .

Still according to Brantner et al . (2008), the use of services based on *Utility Computing* is equally significant for providers, in the sense that

If there is a need to use third-party services , they will be obliged to pay only the equivalent for their use of what they actually receive, eliminating initial investments in IT infrastructure. However, it is worth noting that in general, cloud environments require the ability to support a high rate of data reading and writing processes, in addition to updates and analysis.

These premises lead to the conclusion that users are moving their data to the cloud and can thus interact with it in a simple way and regardless of access location. It is worth, within this context, to present some more details on the subject of *Cloud Computing* .

2.1.5.1 Cloud Computing Service Models

Mell and Grance (2011) identify three architectural patterns for service models in cloud computing . Are they:

a) Infrastructure as a Service (IaaS) - Means the provisioning of virtual servers and other devices, intended by the user and charged by factors, such as the number of virtual servers and amount of data stored or transmitted, in addition to other components. Therefore, it is up to the user to only hire the fundamental computing resources for the implementation of their activities, operating systems and applications.

b) *Software* as a Service (SaaS) - System where the cloud provider provides the user with any application , system or software, which is in turn deployed in the cloud. It is a model where the acquisition and/or use of software is not related to the purchase of licenses.

c) Platform as a Service (PaaS) - Refers to a service model, provided by the cloud provider, which is between SaaS and IaaS, aiming to make the use of resources more flexible. It allows the use of software and the development of own (user) applications . The user does not control the server infrastructure (network, storage and systems), but can control the deployed applications and configurations of the cloud environment.

2.1.5.2 Cloud Computing Deployment Models

models , according to Mell and Grance (2011), symbolize the arrangement of cloud computing environments and classify them as follows:

a) Private cloud - In this model, all cloud infrastructure belongs and is controlled by an exclusive organization or entity, with its structure located within the company itself or outsourced elsewhere;

b) Public cloud - This means when the cloud infrastructure is made available to the general public , with control falling over an organization also responsible for its commercialization. In this format, any user can benefit from the services provided by the cloud, simply by knowing how to access it;

c) cloud - Proposes a shared infrastructure format. The cloud infrastructure is shared by more than one organization with common interests; It is

d) Hybrid cloud - this model occurs when the cloud infrastructure is a composition of two or more previous models, connected through standardized technology.

In this sense, Vieira et al. (2012) highlight that the use of cloud computing to use *NoSQL* databases is already a reality for companies like Google Facebook, IBM, Twitter among others, to implement analytical processing of *logs* , *posts* , web traffic and other tasks that make use of high scalability, high availability, writing and reading with low latency, storage efficient and quick access in real time, in addition to being considered an efficient and low-cost way.

Cloud computing models can help accelerate the potential for scalable analytics solutions . Clouds offer flexibility and efficiency to access data, deliver *insights* and drive value. In this context, it is

measure the close relationship between the characteristics of cloud computing and the parameterization of *Big Data data* and, therefore, also on unstructured data .

2.2 Unstructured data

The amount of data generated daily in various digital domains in the order of terabytes/petabytes/zettabytes implies, as previously mentioned, new and complex challenges in the form of manipulation, storage, treatment and use of queries in the most diverse areas of computing, especially with regard to information retrieval (CUZZOCREA , 2011).

From this perspective, and with the need to manage data whose formats are difficult to accommodate in relational systems, the use of traditional database management systems (DBMS) is considered inappropriate for dealing with these, now going by the pseudonym " *Big Data* ", imposing needs such as: executing queries with low latency, processing large volumes of data, scalability, support for flexible data storage models, and simple support for data replication and distribution .

To solve the various problems and challenges generated by *Big Data ,* the movement called *NoSQL* (*Not only SQL*) emerges as a trend , predestined to provide innovative solutions for storing and processing large volumes of data, which for the most part require a scalar architecture, easy, horizontal, where new data can be inserted efficiently, coexisting harmoniously with cloud environments (AGRANAL, 2011). Companies such as Google and Facebook, considered large data generators, already use them for the analytical processing of logs, queries, conventional insertions , among countless other tasks regarding their data. Likewise, there are examples of financial institutions , government agencies , *and commerce* . This proves to us the existence of great demands for solutions that perform on different complex data models, with flexibility, scalability and support.

Currently a reference for non- relational databases , the term *NoSQL* It originates chronologically from 1998. On this occasion, by not using SQL language in data query programs, Carlo Strozzi created the term that he first called "Strozzi SQL". The term was used again later in 2009 at a conference organized by Johan Oskarsson about *open source* databases with the name " *NoSQL meetup* " (ABRAMOVA et al . , 2014).

NoSQL technology emerged due to the need to efficiently process large volumes of data, given its exponential growth over the last few years and because this is an equally future trend . The aforementioned authors also argue that the use of this technology in new systems gives them more flexibility than traditional relational database models, as they are not tied into rigid schemes , are distributed, scalable and have better performance, in addition to of not needing a robust infrastructure to store their data.

In turn, Google, through an article published in 2006 under the title " *BigTable: A Distributed Storage System for Structured Data* ", once again emerges the term *NoSQL as a data processing proposal, with the promise of being a* scalable database and fault tolerant, very fast query , as it already indexed the data as soon as it was inserted into the database.

Thus, a new concept for data processing was disseminated, a concept that immediately fell into favor with *open source* communities , which began to develop numerous non- relational database solutions .

Associating these factors with the need to provide information through data whose formats did not fit into traditional relational systems, spread across multiple servers and in a significantly large and exponential quantity, they corroborated in factual terms the effective emergence of *NoSQL* databases .

fast and efficient data processing , prioritizing performance, and leaving aside the relational patterns of old models. According to Leavitt (2010), these prerogatives make it possible to store and retrieve data quickly and efficiently, regardless of its structure and content.

NoSQL databases have a fault-tolerant distributed architecture , which is based on distributing data across several servers. If a server stops working, the system will remain operational, thus ensuring high levels of availability.

Another important *NoSQL* feature is horizontal scalability, which consists of increasing the number of machines in the system, dividing data processing according to the needs of the system, in order to always obtain high levels of performance. It is worth noting that, when a system "scales" horizontally, it adds more nodes to the system, a new computer to the *cluster* . On the other hand, vertically scaling a system implies aggregating processing resources, memory or disk, for example, to a single node.

Flexibility and simplistic manipulation also characterize non- relational databases . They denote simplicity in their manipulation and configuration, while they do not have a deterministic scheme , as in SQL DBMS, which facilitates the distribution of data between several servers, each one being responsible for a part of the data to be worked on.

2.2.1 Characteristics of *NoSQL* Databases

To try to describe the characteristics of *NoSQL* technology for data processing, it is first necessary to remember their heritage with regard to the term *Big Data* . Invariably the association between *Big Data* and *NoSQL* , regarding their functional adjectives regarding data processing, is unique to them. However, a more peculiar detail below is necessary.

It is initially worth considering that the CAP Theorem (*Consistency, Availability, and Partition Tolerance*), as stated by Souza (2010), portrays the three requirements that affect distributed systems :

    a) consistency - the system is ready to be used immediately after inserting a record ;

    b) availability - the system remains active over a period of time; and c) fault tolerance - the system is capable of functioning in the event of failure of its components.

According to the author, and based on the aforementioned theorem, it is not possible, in a distributed data system , for these three requirements to coexist. It is possible to have two of them simultaneously, and the choice of which of these will be directly related to the requirements imposed. These paradigms form the conceptual infrastructure for the Basically *Available, Eventual, Consistency* model that is used by *NoSQL* databases . From this new perspective, it is suggested that there will be no updates for a certain period of time and, in the meantime, all pending updates will be propagated across all system nodes , making the system consistent.

Furthermore , there are numerous characteristics that can be fully assessed when trying to reveal the behavior of *NoSQL* databases . However, some of them stand out and shine through in terms of their adjectives. According to Näsholm (2012), most unstructured databases share a collection of characteristics , and may present some exceptions due to the broad context in which they fit. From a generalized perspective, they would be:

a) Scalability (horizontal) – Scalability implies that it is possible to expand a data storage system, without incurring additional costs, or at the lowest possible cost . In this sense, it expresses being able to handle an increasing workload evenly, that is, being able to grow and expand. A scale-out system is autonomous to add more nodes to the *cluster* system , such as a new

computer or processing device, while a system that has vertical scalar characteristics , adds resources to a single node, by increasing memory or physical space , for example. Theoretically, no limits are imposed on the number of nodes in a *cluster* , what is attributed to it is a notion of reality and investment. According to Pritchett (2008):

> When a relational database grows beyond the capacity of a single node, it is necessary to choose vertical or horizontal scalability. Vertical scalability is not an option for systems that handle large volumes of data. Thus, the option is to scale horizontally. (PRITCHETT, 2008)

NoSQL databases have a common peculiarity: eventual consistency. This characteristic that is also attributed to them is essential for success in achieving high levels of scalability;

b) Large Volumes – the main proposal of *NoSQL systems* is to meet the requirements for managing large volumes of data on a scale that is unlikely to be successful if traditional databases are adopted;

c) Distributed - Distributed systems form the basis of processing and storage of *NoSQL* databases . Replicating data across countless nodes and servers is a key factor in the success of a system that aims for redundancy and high availability;

d) Most *NoSQL* databases are "simple" in terms of use and configuration. It means that all of its functions are easily accessible from the perspective of common use by another system (PALMER, 2010). The MongoDB data processing system [36], which uses the JSON format [37], is an example of such a statement. Following the policy described here, it is not necessary to hire database specialists to manage *NoSQL databases* , this task being the responsibility of the developers;

e) *NoSQL* Databases are free from the imposition of a scheme. They do not denote a fixed structure or standardization for the storage of unstructured data , maintaining a performance considered acceptable for the requirements of *Big Data systems* . Contrary to what SQL databases mean, this approach facilitates the distribution of data between several nodes, where each of these nodes is responsible for "taking care" of just a slice of the total data. This way, customers are able to store data in the form they choose, without following a pre-defined structure , as they would do in relational databases;

f) BASE*Eventually consistent*) . While ACID creates difficulties in developing databases in the distributed model, BASE has characteristics of being available,

---

[36] https://www.mongodb.com/
[37] *JavaScript Object Notation* - JavaScript Object Notation - www.json.org

lightweight and consistent, in addition to being tolerant to temporary inconsistencies when prioritizing availability; It is

g) Availability - A high availability system is a system capable of resisting failures and keeping services active for as long as possible. It also involves high memory management and processing capacity inherent to the responses required by system requests , with optimized response time.

2.2.2 *NoSQL* databases

Different approaches are used to classify *NoSQL* databases . However, within this new class of technologies, it is correct to infer that non- relational databases are classified into Key-Value Schema Databases (*Key-Value-based*), Document-Oriented Databases (*Document-*

based), Column-oriented databases (*Column-based*) and Graph-oriented databases (*Graph-based*).

2.2.2.1 Key-Value Databases

They are characterized as the simplest and from which the best performance is obtained among the other types. Uses a key for each field and a value and in the form of *hash tables* distributed (DHT). Your content can be stored in any data format. In practice , a set of algorithms or matrices are used to search all data in shared files, where access to this data is always carried out using its primary and unique key (ABRAMOVA e. al., 2014).

Due to its main advantage of good horizontal scalability and high performance, the Key-Value model is used mainly in applications where data changes occur with high frequency, and is not recommended for applications inherent to high complexity queries, due to its low indexing capacity . The nodes are programmed to find specific subjects in files and bring them up as a search result.

The most well-known Key-Value databases, so to speak, in the commercial *NoSQL data environment* they are Riak [38], Dynamite, Redis [39], Amazon DynamoDB [40], Azure Table Storage, Berkeley DB [41], and even Cassandra (even though it has column-oriented properties).

2.2.2.2 Document-Oriented Databases

These types of databases provide storage in the form of sets of documents and are based on key-value pairs, having a highly flexible scheme. Because it has a different schema than other databases

NoSQL , in the sense that each document is made up of a set of fields stored in an unstructured way, identified and associated by a unique key, the document-oriented database model is superior in terms of the form of queries, as allows queries in the form of sets of documents, with order or restrictions on the results. As it is considered the most

---

[38]basho.com
[39] https://redis.io/
[40] https://aws.amazon.com/pt/dynamodb/
[41] www.oracle.com

versatile database , they are ideal options for processing semi-structured data, stored in a standard format, such as XML [42], JSON [43] or BSON [44]. According to Kuznetsov & Poskonin (2014), they are appropriate for problems where one is not sure of the type of data to be investigated and worked on, where performance is irrelevant and the main focus is on the premise of good performance when querying this data. and in the storage of large volumes.

For Kaur et al . (2013), the way of working at the expense of complexity associated with high scalability, whether for structured, semi-structured or unstructured data, is one of its main advantages over other models. Under the eyes of Abramova et al . (2014), systems such as CouchDB and MongoDB represent, in a practical application context , a great choice for working with large quantities of documents that are stored in files such as XML, text documents, emails, electronic commerce systems on the Internet, among others with the same characteristics.

2.2.2.3 Column-Oriented Databases

It is a model considered capable of supporting large amounts of data. In relation to the Key-Value model, it presents greater complexity, due to the fact that the orientation passes from records to the form of columns where not all lines have the same number of columns and, yes, a line corresponds to a set of columns associated with the same primary key , which makes writing a new registration. This translates into less computational effort , increasing system performance.

According to Abramova et al . (2014), the column-oriented database model is ideal for systems that converge to the treatment of complex and large-volume data structures, a statement supported by the characteristic that columns can be stored by column families , with the purpose to facilitate the organization and distribution of data. In practice, they are ideal on occasions where the number of writing operations (*write*) is greater than the number of reading operations (*read*), which is the case in systems with a high number of requests.

Cassandra and Hbase form the main duo to exemplify this database model, followed by others such as BigTable (Google) [45], Hypertable [46], Infobright [47] and even Riak.

2.2.2.4 Graph-oriented Databases

Graph databases are considered the most complex, primarily due to the fact that they store objects and not records like the others, where the search for data is done through navigation through these objects , storing edges and vertices as a representation of the association that these same data have each other (ALVARES, *et.al* , 2016).

Considered ideal for dealing with data from social networks and also useful as a tool for extracting data to build competitive knowledge between companies, graph-oriented databases have the capacity to store information obtained through the relationship between

---

[42] **XML** (*and Xtensible Markup Language)* is a W3C recommendation for generating markup languages *for* special needs . Creates a single infrastructure for different languages.
[43] **JSON** (*JavaScript Object* Notation) is a lightweight data exchange format that is easy to interpret and generate. It is based on a subset of the JavaScript programming language .
[44] **BSON** (Binary JSON) is a binary way to represent simple data structures, associative arrays (called objects or documents in MongoDB), and various data types of specific interest to MongoDB.
[45] https://cloud.google.com/bigtable/
[46] hypertable.org
[47] http://www.infobright.com

nodes, in addition to do not have a previously defined structure.

Its functional architecture is based on the use of nodes and edges to represent stored data, with nodes containing properties in the form of Key-Value pairs and relationships always having an associated name and a direction containing a sender node and a recipient node , very useful for storing information in models with many relationships (ROBINSON et al . , 2013).

Neo4j [48], HyperGraphDB [49], AllegroGraph [50]and VertexDB [51], are examples of graph-oriented databases.

A framework or classification regarding the form of the database, with the purpose of exposing the large number of existing options , can also be found and detailed in other literary sources, which are not currently relevant.

2.2.3 Haddop

In the context *of Big Data* , which encompasses a very large volume of data, the use of a mechanism to store information across multiple machines is essential. The Apache Hadoop project, created by Doug Cutting [52], is one of the best-known solutions for *Big Data* today. It is a high-performance, fault-tolerant system for storing and processing data, in the form of an *open source* solution licensed by Apache, for distributed, scalable and secure computing . Its purpose is to offer an infrastructure for storing and processing large volumes of data, providing linear scalability and fault tolerance , thus allowing the storage and processing of large data in a distributed environment between computer *clusters through the use of* simplified programming methods . According to White (2012), Hadoop has been breaking records both in the aggregation of machines in the *cluster* and in processing speeds.

In Hadoop, high availability is not the responsibility of the *hardware* . In it, the detection of failures that may eventually occur, even because the machines in the *cluster* are subject to error, it is done in the application layer . Its services are supported by two main agents: the File System

Distributed Hadoop (HDFS), responsible for storing data, with notable reliability, and Hadoop *MapReduce* , responsible for high-performance processing of this data. Immediately here, more detail about these artifacts is necessary.

2.2.4 HDFS

In the format of a subproject of the Apache Hadoop project (*Apache Software Foundation*), we can synthetically conceptualize the *Hadoop Distributed File System* (HDFS), as a file system used in the processing of data in the Hadoop ecosystem. As previously measured, Hadoop is ideal for storing large amounts of data, ranging in terabytes and petabytes, it allows storing and processing large data in a distributed environment between *clusters* of computers using simple programming models and, therefore, it is HDFS

---

[48] https://neo4j.com
[49] hypergraphdb.org
[50] https://allegrograph.com
[51] www.vertex.com
[52] Chief Architect at Cloudera, Inc. Advisor at Proximal Labs, Inc. Founded the Apache Hadoop, Nutch and Lucene projects.

that Hadoop uses as a storage system.

HDFS provides connectivity between computers (cluster nodes) *through* which data files are distributed. It is permissible to access and store the data files in a continuous format and the executable parts of the system as well as commands are executed following the *MapReduce* paradigms (described later). This system stores so-called metadata in different locations than the application data. This metadata is stored on a server specifically designated for this function and is called *NameNode* . On the other hand, the application data is recorded on other servers outside the first and are called *DataNodes* . Both servers communicate following rules based on the TCP protocol. Quam (2000) advises that metadata is defined as attributes that describe data, at a higher level of abstraction than data, used to describe the origin or provenance of a certain set of data.

HDFS is highly fault tolerant and is plausible for use on "simple", low-cost computers. It achieves this through the replication of file blocks, specified by the application in the quantity it deems appropriate. *NameNode* is responsible for replication . Data integrity is ensured by checksum validation on HDFS file contents by storing calculated checksums in separate, hidden files in the same NameSpace *as* the actual data. The HDFS *NameSpace* is stored using a transaction log maintained by each *NameNode* . Figure 6 shows, architecturally, the way HDFS works.

Figure 6: HDFS Architecture

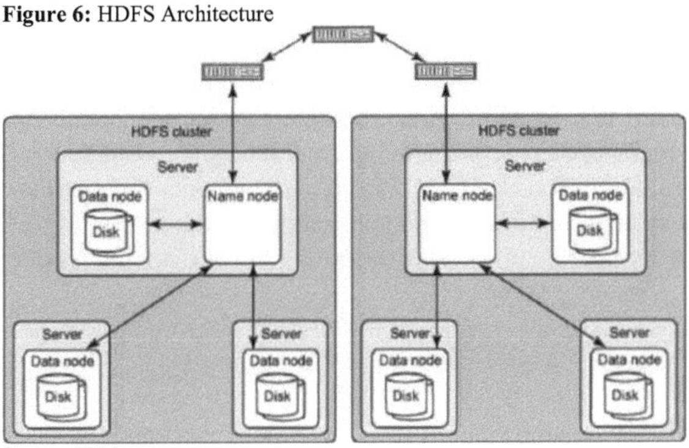

Source IBM.com

2.2.5 *MapReduce*

The large increase in volume and variety of *Big Data data* has caused significant difficulties in terms of the ability to process data into useful information of this nature. To solve this processing bottleneck, Lin and Dyer (2010) suggest that the only plausible alternative to solving this setback comes from applying the divide and conquer paradigm. Strategically means partitioning a large imbroglio into slices of smaller problems. This initially characterizes the emergence of the applicable concept of *MapReduce* .

Still citing White (2012), *MapReduce* can be defined as a programming paradigm aimed at batch processing *of* large volumes of data across several machines, obtaining results in a reasonable time. The concept of distributed programming is used to solve problems, adopting the strategy of dividing them into smaller and independent problems.

MapReduce It is arranged together with a distributed file system, specially designed to support applications that need to process large volumes of data. Conceptualizing

MapReduce a little more , Paiva and Revoredo (2016), drawing on the work of Dean and Ghemawat, highlight that:

> *MapReduce is a parallel programming model for large volumes of data. It is inspired by the divide and conquer strategy , but abstracts from the programmer the complexity of problems typical of managing distributed applications, allowing the developer to dedicate himself solely to solving the problem to be addressed, leaving the application to perform distribution and parallelism. . (PAIVA, REVOREDO, 2016)*

MapReduce working model makes use of computer *clusters* to process tasks, distributing them among nodes. Each node is effectively a machine in the *cluster* , being assigned the adjective "master" or "slave". Master nodes are tasked with managing the processing actually performed by slave nodes .

In a practical reference, according to Dean and Ghemawat (2004), the function of the *Map* operator is to divide the initial problem into smaller groups, which will be delivered to the other nodes in the *cluster* . In contrast, the *Reduce* operation retains for itself the task of processing the information initially originating from the data groups delivered by the *Map* function , thus providing an answer to the original problem. Unlike SQL, *MapReduce processes* store data persistently for later querying . White (2012) complements by emphasizing that task processing is divided into three different stages: the " *map* " stage, the " *reduce* " stage , which are accessible to the programmer, and an intermediate stage called " *shuffle* ", created by the system at run time. execution.

According to Dean and Ghemawat (2010), *MapReduce* does not require renowned programmers in the construction of distributed systems , on the contrary, it allows programmers with no experience in this specific area, creating systems capable of processing large amounts of data. Tasks related to scheduling, interaction between servers and fault tolerance , for example, are the responsibility of *MapReduce* , maintaining greater focus during the construction of the system, focused on the part relating to the processing of the data itself. Figure 7 and Figure 8 summarize processing according to the map and reduce paradigm.

Figure 7: Processing according to *MapReduce*

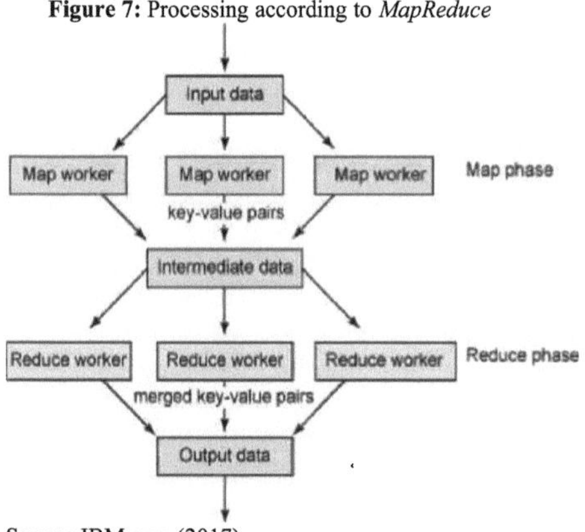

Source IBM.com (2017)
Figure 8: *MapReduce* example

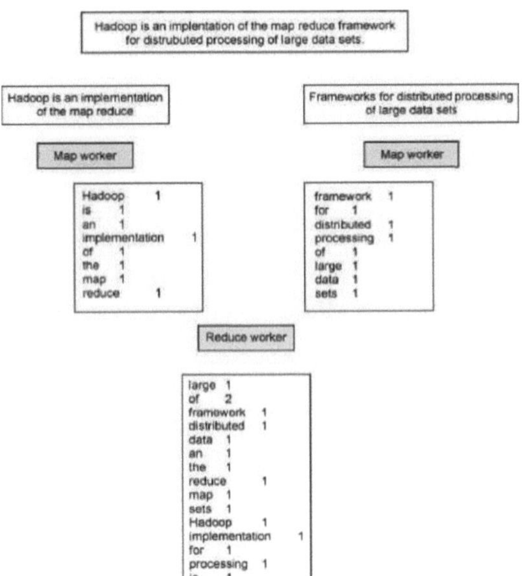

Source IBM.com (2017)

2.2.6 *NoSQL* Architectures

Structured data storage standards have been widely disseminated in the technological environment for decades, are present and are commonly used by institutions in various segments. However, the current technological moment allows, in addition to traditional structured data, exemplified by tables in SQL databases, semi-structured data and especially unstructured data , under the pseudonym *NoSQL* , to be in evidence. Storing, processing and leveraging results from unstructured data requires a different approach than what was previously implemented . Text files, *logs* , videos, images, audio *streaming* , and many others become part of the context of data analysis .

Handling unstructured data , beyond what the file system itself does , requires new architectures. The most significant examples for These architectures are found in the Hadoop ecosystem and in the *MapReduce algorithm* (both of which receive special attention separately in this book).

When using architectures composed of, for example, Hadoop, *MapReduce , NoSQL* databases , *Data Warehouse* [53], together and not separately, working with *Big Data* is characterized .

Meier (2013) makes it possible to show architectural features presented in the implementation of companies such as Facebook, LinkedIn and Oracle. Facebook collects structured and flow-based data from users, which is applied for batch-based data analysis , as shown in Figure 9.

---

[53] Digital data store used to store detailed information regarding a company.

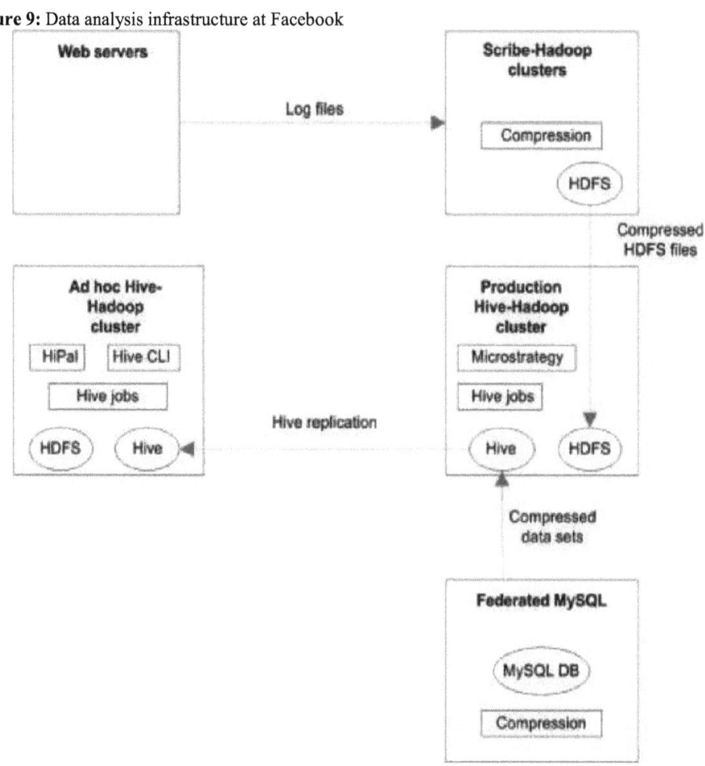

Source: Pääkkönen and Daniel Pakkala (2016)

The same author, through Figure 10, shows that LinkedIn also collects structured and unstructured data , which are analyzed in web environments. development and production and provides services to end users based on data analysis .

Figure 10: Data analytics infrastructure at LinkedIn

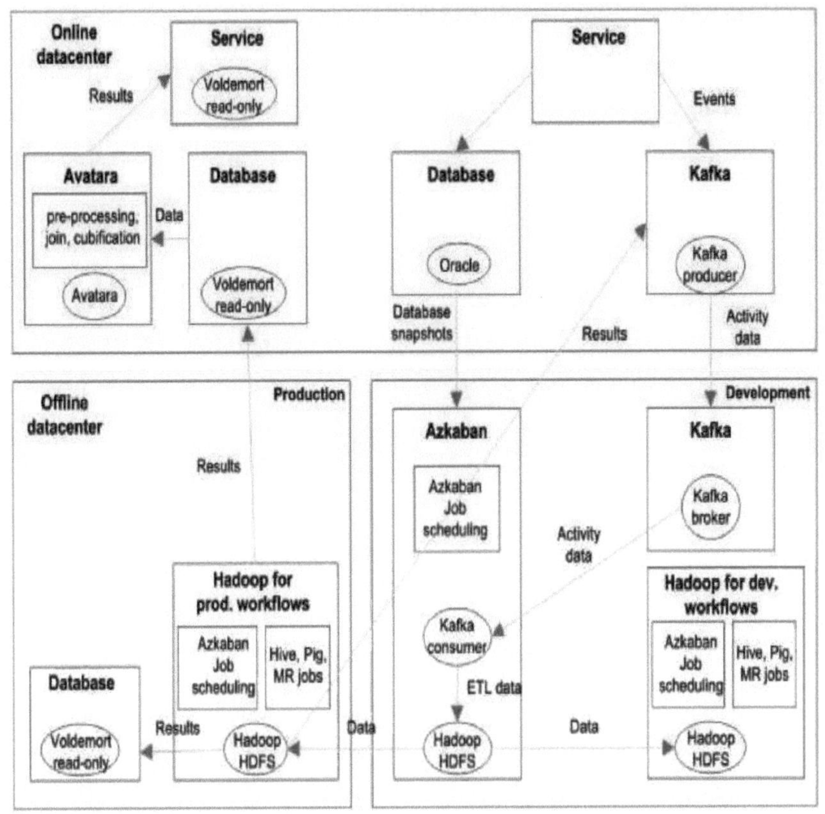

Source : Pääkkönen and Daniel Pakkala (2016)

Twitter [54]primarily deals with *tweets* , which have real-time processing requirements. Netflix[55] is a commercial video streaming service for end users that collects, processes and analyzes user events in *online* , *offline environments* , as well as real -time data analysis , seen through Figure 11.

[54] https://twitter.com
[55] https://www.netflix.com/br

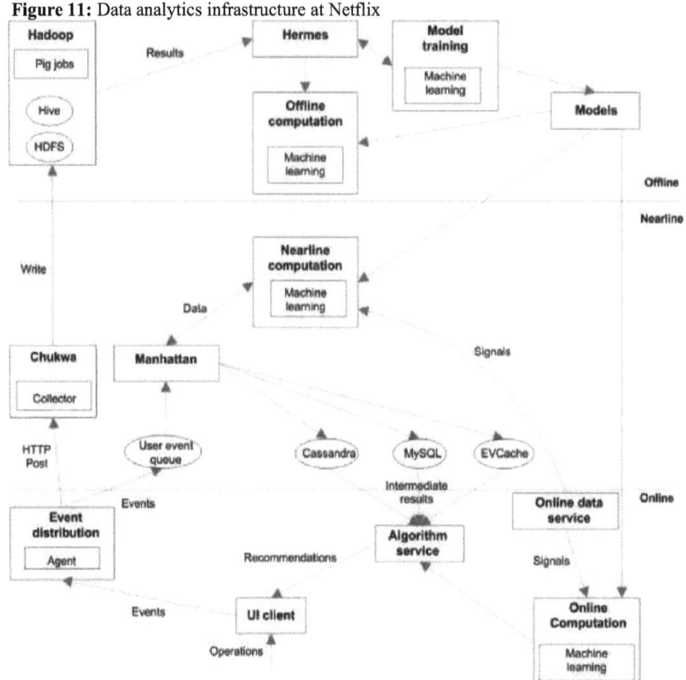

Source : Pääkkönen and Daniel Pakkala (2016)

2.2.7 Lambda Architecture

already been mentioned here, in a pertinent topic , that conventional data processing systems, when it comes to processing large volume data, with frequent updates , end up becoming complex, almost impossible to provide scalability in addition to being more susceptible to human errors. Likewise, the requirements of variety, volume and speed, which are inherent to the design of *Big Data systems,* have also been discussed .

Taking this scenario as a premise, the Lambda architecture emerges , which, according to Marz and Warren (2015), is an architecture that forms the basis for building *Big Data* systems , in the form of a series of layers. Each layer is assigned the function of satisfying a subset of properties based on the functionality of the lower layer. Systems must then be able to handle, in speeds close to real time, with a huge volume of data, coming from varied and distinct sources.

More specifically, the Lambda architecture is divided into three layers, seen in Figure 12: *batch layer* , *speed layer* and *serving layer* and several technologies can be given as an example of the use of this architecture in implementing a *Big Data system* . For example: Kafka for data distribution , Hadoop and Spark in the *batch layer* , Spark or Storm for real-time data processing and *NoSQL databases* such as HBase or Cassandra in the *speed layer* and for integration in the *serving layer* .

It goes back to Nathan Marz, while working at Twitter, the creation of a generic architecture proposing that the same mass of data will give rise to independent flows of analysis, with the first – called " *batch layer* ", responsible for persisting the data (a database of *NoSQL* data or in a distributed file system) and the second – called " *serving layer* ", responsible for carrying out analyzes on this data, making it available from more than one perspective. On the other hand, this procedure coexists with a layer called " *speed layer* ", which creates real-time analyzes and both layers can provide simultaneous queries. The main characteristic of Lamba architecture is the ambiguity and importance of its layers. They complete each other.

Figure 12: Lambda Architecture

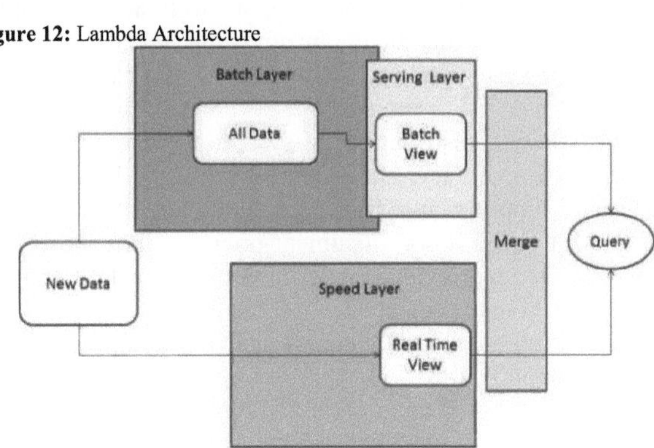

Source: Bar (2016)

2.2.8 *Big Data* and *NoSQL* Technologies and Tools Available

Big Data and *NoSQL* are viewed from two perspectives: infrastructure and " *Analytics*" , *highlighting as an example the NoSQL* databases for the latter and Hadoop associated with *MapReduce* , for the first mentioned.

Big Data ecosystem It is composed of technologies: ingestion, storage, processing, messaging, reference libraries and machine learning library .

It is worth mentioning below, even briefly, some technologies – in the form of *software tools* /systems, considered of greater importance in the current context of *Big Data* , as well as in the processing of unstructured data . Highlighting that, at the existential level in the market, countless other tools and applications are able to process non- relational data . The intention here, for now, is to provide a broad view of the topic, and not just the choice of this or that solution to implement any project.

a) **Flume -** is an efficient distributed system for collecting large volumes of log data service efficiently and reliably. It uses a simple model that allows *online* analytical application (Apache, 2017). It follows a flexible, fault-tolerant architecture and, according to Hoffman (2013), its three main components are: sources, communication channel and *sink* . After going through these, the files can then be distributed in a non-relational format , in a system of distributed files ;

b) **Sqoop -** is a tool that allows data transfer between relational databases and the Hadoop platform (Apache, 2017). It was created for the purpose of efficiently transferring large data packets between Hadoop HDFS and relational database systems such as MySQL [56], Oracle or PostgreSQL [57];

c) **Kafka** - is a distributed log messaging software suitable for use in *offline* and *online modes* . It is designed to allow a single *cluster* to serve as the data backbone and can be expanded elastically;

d) **RabbitMQ** - is an *open source* messaging server system that supports multiple configuration options , clustering and high availability (RabbitMq, 2017);

e) **Cassandra - Lakshman and Malik (2010) define Cassandra as a** distributed storage system for managing large volumes of data through numerous *clusters* , with high availability, consistency and scalability, as well as low implementation and administration costs . Its fault tolerance – *by* not being linked to a single possible point of failure , it increases system reliability, as data is replicated across several cluster nodes ;

f) **Hadoop HDFS** - It is a distributed file system and the most important object of Hadoop. It is not a tool or library, but it is the core of the Hadoop platform. It offers high performance and supports large files. It is fault tolerant;

g) **MongoDB** - MongoDB is a document-oriented data processing system for complex data queries and aggregations . It supports replication and sharding and has become very popular among its features;

h) **HBase** - It is a column-oriented database and was built to provide requests with low latency under Hadoop HDFS;

i) **Elastic** - Tool for distributed text queries . It has a fast search time as it works with indexes;

j) **Yarn** – *Yet Another Resource Negotiator* is a *framework* that represents the next generation of Hadoop. It is responsible for controlling the *cluster 's resources* ; k) **Tableau** - It is a proprietary data visualization and analysis platform (it has free versions);

l) **Mesos** - Mesos is a distributed system for managing the resources of a *cluster* developed by the University of Berkeley system. Can reference up to ten thousand nodes;

m) **Hadoop *MapReduce*** - It is the implementation of Hadoop *MapReduce* . Designed to work on HDFS and with parallel processing on the map and reduce paradigm. As it makes intense use of the disk, it decreases system performance, yet it is one of the most important data processing structures ever created;

n) **Spark** - An *open source system, with* a parallel processing structure for cluster computing aiming to analyze data in the fastest way possible. Developed with a focus on speed and ease of use, always aiming for sophisticated analysis . It is memory intensive making it up to a hundred times faster than Hadoop *MapReduce* ;

o) **Storm** - Apache Storm is a *framework* for developing distributed data stream processing applications . Driven by Twitter, it has *a design* aimed at processing events extremely quickly (more than one million records per second/node);

p) **Flink** - It is a recent *framework* for processing *streaming* with high performance and low latency;

q) **Spark Mllib** - Spark MLlib is a framework that includes machine learning algorithms leveraging the benefits of distributed computing and memory-intensive work . It includes classification, regression and clustering algorithms;

r) **Hive** - The Hive [55] started as a subproject of the Hadoop project. Provides a set of

---

[56] https://www.mysql.com
[57] https://www.postgresql.org

tools to read, write and manage Hadoop data through an SQL-like syntax;

s) **Pig** - Pig [56] is a platform for data analysis that consists of a high- level language for expressing data analysis and the infrastructure for executing this language;

t) **Spark SQL -** It is a module included in Spark to work with structured data using SQL syntax, but taking advantage of execution in the Spark core ;

u) **R -** Environment for statistical analysis;

v) **D3 -** It is a JavaScript library for data visualization ;

x) **Mahout -** It is an *Apache Software Foundation project* to produce free implementations of scalable machine learning algorithms ;

y) **Talend -** Under the open standards of the *General Public License* (GPL), it presents itself as an *Open source tool* for ETL (Extraction, Transformation and Loading) and stable, solid and innovative data integration , with a graphical interface based on components;

z) **Knime -** It is a good data mining tool . Enterprise - grade , easy-to-implement open source platform ;

aa) **Pentaho -** It is an *open source platform* with a powerful architecture for creating solutions for BI (Business *Intelligence*) needs . The tool was developed in Java, previously considered one of the best *software* for business intelligence . Supports ETL (*Extraction, Transformation and Load*), reports, *workflow* , OLAP (*Online Analytical Processing*) and data mining with *Data-mining* and *Big Data* ;

ab) **MySQL -** Produced by Oracle® [57] , it is an open source database system with proven performance, reliability and ease of use,
especially when database option for web-based applications;

ac) **Redis -** Redis is an *open source* data structure tool for in -memory storage. Used as a database, cache and message broker. It supports data structures such as strings , *hashes* , lists, sets, *logs* , among others;

ad) **Qlik View Sense Desktop -** *Open source* tool designed for data visualization , which allows you to create interactive reports and *dashboards* with tables and graphs;

ae) **Weka - The Weka** (*Waikato Environment for Knowledge Analysis)* software , licensed under the *General Public License,* is a tool that applies Machine Learning *concepts* to computational and statistical data analysis through data mining , seeking to generate solutions, based on the inductions that these same data generate; It is

af) **Neo4j -** *Open source* tool , is a graph-oriented *NoSQL* database suitable for working with a large amount of data (*Big Data*). It has ACID and *Clustering support* , in addition to adding speed by working with data in memory. Considered a great tool for working with social media data.

Subsequent to these descriptions (collected from the official websites of each of those mentioned), the illustration in Figure 13 suggests, through a quick visual conception, a greater identification of the tools and solution, in terms of the field of action. The choice of some tools, aggregates, can form a practical solution for processing *NoSQL data* , for which they were described here.

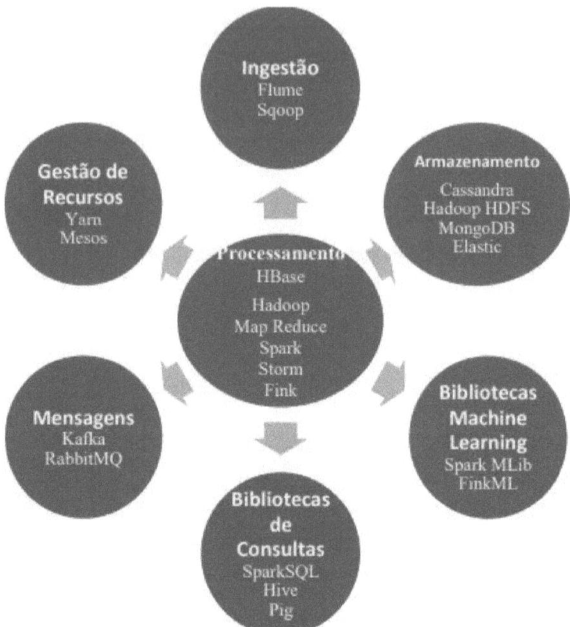

Figure 13: *Big Data* tools in accordance with the area of activity
Source: Prepared by the author (2017)

It is estimated that the global *Big Data market* it will be worth 88 billion dollars by 2021 [58]. With this prospect, it is not enough for institutions to just be interested in using *Big Data* , analyzing data in large quantities or with different structures, they need to be able to translate the data. What to do with the volume and variety of data? What do they mean? How to analyze them in real time? What knowledge or improvements can this bring to institutional management ? These and many other unknowns seek answers from the data scientist.

This requires knowledge and appropriate mastery of data processing, business vision and programming skills (databases), in addition, obviously, understanding and mastering the various *Big Data platforms* . Must be able to translate data into management information and have the analytical capacity to identify valuable information based on *Big Data tools* . Therefore, knowing *hardware* and software tools for data collection and analysis , such as Hadoop (open source) is also an inherent activity.

2.2.9 *NoSQL* in Context *Pen Source* and Free Licenses

In order to use all this data generated in the *NoSQL context* , and extract information from it, it is necessary to use special tools for storage, extraction, analysis, formatting and visualization. At the user level , the market offers paid solutions that promise to satisfactorily satisfy (in the supplier's view) these premises. However, the *open source* community is also included in this proposition, through technically effective projects, such

---

[58] http://www.cienciaedados.com/big-data-como-servico/

as those provided by the Apache Foundation [59].

The biggest advantage of *free* [60]/*open-source* applications is the possibility of minimizing, or even eliminating, TCO (Total *Cost* of Ownership) (YANG, 2016). The *Open Source* movement offers robust and professional database solutions for almost all types of applications and problems.

Considering also that when it comes to cutting costs, those responsible for IT solutions in institutions can resort to adopting an *open source model* , with no licensing fee. However, it is worth remembering that this requires procedures and incentives in training and product maintenance , responsibility for installations and necessary updates.

Based on this scenario, it is worth viewing in Table 1 a brief list of some *free/open source* tools capable of being used in the functional basis of a reference architecture, the objective of this work:

Table 1: *Free/open source* tools for data processing

Data base	Input data	Processing Distributed	Data analysis	Data visualization
MongoDB Cassandra Neo4j Hbase MySQL Spark SQL	Kafka Sqoop Talend Flume	Apache Hadoop/HDFS Hive Impala Pig Redis Pentaho Knime Yarn Spark Storm Redis	R Pentaho Elastic Mahout Knime Weka	Qlik View Tableau

Source: Prepared by the author (2017)

2.3 Related work

The staged demonstration of reference architectures, as well as the use of free *software* for collecting and processing *Big Data* and unstructured data , are present in architectures from other institutions or companies.

The research entitled " *Towards a Big Data Reference Architecture* " (MAIER, 2013), consists of an approach to current technologies, which can be used to implement a

---

[59] www.apache.org/foundation/
[60] No licensing or usage costs.

reference architecture , built from traditional companies. It shows that the implementation of components with technologies such as the Apache Hadoop ecosystem and the so-called " *NoSQL* " databases can compose a reference architecture. The proposed reference architecture and a survey of the state of the art can, according to the research, guide designers in the creation of unstructured data processing systems for decision making.

The aforementioned research by Maier (2013) positively confirms that the research proposal that gives rise to this work receives support that allows the author to construct in an orderly and factual manner a reference architecture, which is compatible with current affairs with regard to a possible implementation, as it specifically addresses *NoSQL* data . However, it is worth noting that this, although plausible for general acceptance , does not mention the reality proposed by this author's research, when it does not refer to the management of educational institutions . A reality notably different from large companies such as those cited by Maier (2013).

research by Pääkkönen and Pakkala (2016), " *Reference Architecture and Classification of Technologies, Products and Services for Big Data Systems* " addresses use cases in *Big Data* by large companies such as Facebook, LinkedIn or Netflix, showing an independent reference architecture of technology for data systems, which is based on the analysis of published implementation architectures.

Regarding the research by Pääkkönen and Pakkala (2016), it should be noted that it has a more focused focus on the treatment of large volumes of data, which in relation to the proposal of this research, does not give due attention to structured data, nor to the "public institution" aspect.

Furthermore, Costa's master's thesis (2015) "BASIS: A *Big Data Architecture* for *Smart Cities* " becomes relevant when he proposes a *Big Data architecture* for *Smart Cities* , creating a conceptual and technological framework, aimed at studying the main existing approaches between the set of scientific publications and *Big Data* technologies that can integrate technological components of an architecture in several layers of abstraction, from the most conceptual to the most technological.

Finally, also mentioning the research by Costa (2015), it is emphasized, although it addresses *open source tools* for data processing and also *NoSQL* data , as well as being very useful as a means of promoting in-depth understanding of the tools available on the market, the concern is focused on IoT. The term IoT is supporting the research proposed in this compendium, but not the main focus.

Therefore, it is suggested that the works cited here deserve attention from the author in order to instigate, from these, complements through additional research, with regard to the processing of unstructured data , the construction of a specific architecture , with a focus on reality of educational institutions , which will ultimately bring to the academic community and the public linked to these institutions, new reference material for use in implementing unstructured data processing systems .

Chapter 3
3 REFERENCE ARCHITECTURE FOR UNSTRUCTURED DATA PROCESSING

In previous chapters, some important technologies were presented for implementing applications that fit into the context of unstructured data . The purpose of chapter two was to bring to light the necessary knowledge so that it is possible to analyze and design solutions based on different scenarios that involve the processing of unstructured and large-volume data. Also, functionalities, data flows and data storage of architectures available in the literature were analyzed. The next step of this work is to propose a reference architecture model . In light of the above, below is a proposed solution to the problem that this work exposes in its initial stage. This procedure will take place through a process that consists of deciding on a type for the reference architecture , selecting a design strategy , empirical data acquisition , construction of the reference architecture and evaluation.

Social networks are no longer used just for leisure and are currently used by citizens to express opinions on the most varied subjects, especially when they refer to social or behavioral issues . Educational institutions can make use of this data, analyze it and apply it to qualify educational management , propose courses , teaching methods, monitor graduates or even obtain an overview of allocation in the job market, among many other actions. In addition to social networks, other data generating vehicles on the Internet can support this role. Processing this information is not a trivial task, as the data, in addition to being different in terms of structure, is generated in large quantities.

An architectural model will be presented with the intention of contemplating the situation described previously. The amount of data generated by the vehicles mentioned also requires a vision focused on the *Big Data* context , as seen in previous chapters , relational databases and other traditional technologies are not suitable for this type of problem. Therefore, this study aims to serve as a vehicle for future implementations, which can handle unstructured data , in the Federal Institutes of Science and Technology Education.

The construction of this reference architecture adopts an empirical method and is based on the analysis of use cases of architectures for processing data published in works on the use of heterogeneous technologies and architectures, which mainly focused on describing architectures of individual contributions such as Facebook (MEIER, 2013) or LinkedIn (SUMBALY, 2013), already mentioned in chapter two. Added to this is the conduct of a study on data processing tools and techniques . This abstract design method and the resulting resulting architecture are intended to facilitate the creation of a more elaborate *design* architecture and the selection of technologies or commercial solutions , to build a system for processing data considered complex. Therefore, the design of the reference architecture for processing unstructured data is presented, built inductively based on cases in the literature.

reference architecture is intended to be useful in the following ways: it should facilitate the creation of other concrete architecture(s); increase understanding of the topic; provide a generic image about the processing of data in different formats; contain the typical functionalities and data flows of the system that is proposed to be built in the future. Said architecture , in summary, as shown in Figure 14, must provide the execution of the following tasks:

a) Extract data related to the educational context (but not only these) posted by social media users ;

b) Extract data related to the educational context (but not only these) found on the Internet;

c) Extract data from systems used by the institution;

d) Provide linear scalability for the number of records that are stored;

e) Analyze and classify content data (*analytic* function – according to the institution 's specific objectives); It is

f) Display a *Dashboard* [61]or web applications to the end user to view the results obtained after the analysis.

Figure 14: Summary of the conceptual aspect of the proposed reference architecture

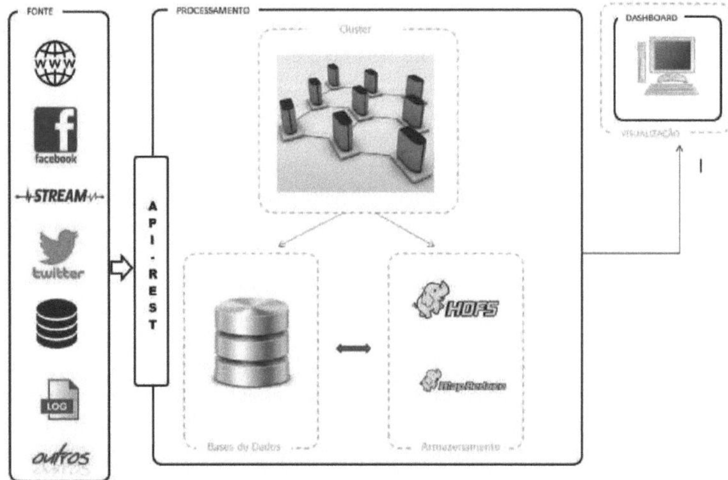

Source: Prepared by the author (2017)

The development of the reference architecture will be explained using two models:

a) **Conceptual Architecture -** describes the levels that constitute the architecture and the explanation of the activities that are carried out at each of the levels. This architecture is presented in Section 3.1.

b) **Functional Architecture -** describes a technological solution , through the instantiation of technologies for each of the levels identified in the conceptual architecture. It should be noted that there may be other technological solutions different from the one presented. This architecture is presented in chapter four.

---

[61] Visual presentation of important information , consolidated and adjusted on one screen for easy monitoring.

3.1 Conceptual Architecture

The proposed architecture is composed of five levels. Each level supports a set of activities associated with it. These range from data collection to the provision of information to the end user , obtained through the analyzes carried out on the data. The levels that subdivide and constitute the architecture, as seen in Figure 15, are:
Source, Acquisition, Processing/Storage, Analysis/Transformation and Visualization.

Figure 15: Reference architecture - high degree of abstraction

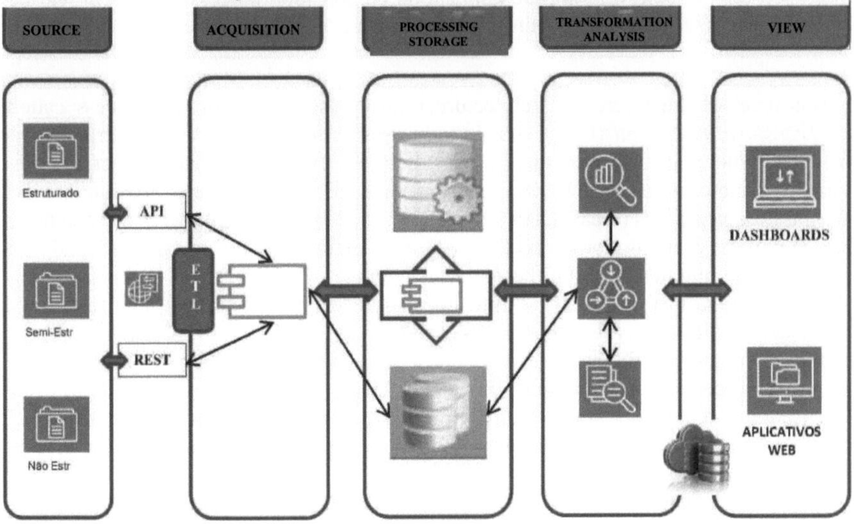

Source: Prepared by the author (2017)

3.1.1 Source

The data sources, represented in both architectures, seek to identify the different sources and types of data that can be used, namely data from social networks, text files, videos, among others, in addition to structured data from local systems, due to the fact that, in small and medium- sized organizations , there is a huge amount of data originating from these sources.

These sources may contain the content of a relational database, which is structured based on any database, information stored from the institution 's proprietary systems , unstructured data , unassociated with a data model, such as content of Web pages or images and semi-structured data, known as irregular or partially structured, such as XML and JSON documents.

3.1.2 Acquisition

Acquisition corresponds to data entry into the system . These will be extracted through available APIs . For example: data extraction and publications from social networks must occur through APIs provided by social networks. The same premise will indicate the acquisition of web content . These tools make it possible to capture public posts through REST services .

REST (*Representational State Transfer*) can be described as an architectural style with constraints applied to components and data elements within a distributed hypermedia web system. Officially defined by W3C [62], REST is not concerned with details of the protocol or component, but rather with its interaction with other components. It is a set of principles that define how *Web Standards* (HTTP [63]and URIs [64]) should be used. By adhering to REST principles during the application composition process , a system will be created that exploits the Web architecture for the benefit of the system itself .

This level of the reference architecture is also responsible for the process called *Extract Transform and Load* (ETL), which comprises actions related to the extraction of data, whether structured, semi-structured or unstructured , from varied and distinct sources, transformation and cleaning (corrections) of them, thus ensuring that these data can later be taken to the storage process (area) (CHAUDHURI et al., 2011). The tasks that this step must perform are: data cleaning; error detection ; data extraction for subsequent analysis; temporary storage in a database. Furthermore, the storage of data that was processed using the ETL process and that will later be used for analytical processing must be a repository capable of storing different types and sources of data.

It is important to add that an ETL flow can be seen as a data pipeline. Data enters at one end of the process in one form and exits in a different and desired form. The complexity of the collection and transformation requirements will depend on the system's objectives and may have up to numerous stages, connecting one or several data sources or running on one or several servers.

When data is extracted, it can be temporarily stored (TEMP database) or transferred and loaded into another storage base that can be called "Raw Data", exclusive for unprocessed data , as suggested by Pääkkönen and Pakkala (2014) . The same procedure can, depending on the functionalities intended by the system, be assigned to streaming data . A process of compressing the extracted data can also improve the efficiency of the transfer and loading processes . The data stored in "Raw Data" can be cleaned or combined and saved to new storage or sent directly to the analysis stage. Cleaning and combining refers to improving the quality of raw, unprocessed data . "Ready Data" can be replicated between data stores. Information extraction refers to storing raw data in a format structured. The repository called "Ready Data" is intended for storing processed and cleaned data.
3.1.3 Processing/Storage

Following the premises of Klein et al. (2016), in the case of a reference architecture, in general terms, the "processing" module must focus its responsibility on the efficient, scalable and reliable execution of the architecture steps. Its functions are: disseminate data throughout the architecture, implement and manage the mechanisms to provide conditions to meet the requirements that the system intends to satisfy, implement and manage the data distribution infrastructure between the *clusters* , provide scalability, obtained through the creation of new data channels when necessary, doing so in the form of distributed and parallel processing. You must also configure and combine other action modules on the data, integrating activities into a cohesive application .

---

[62] The World Wide Web Consortium
[63] Hyper Text Transfer Protocol.
[64] Uniform Resource Identifier.

In relation to distributed processing , it must allow data channels to be distributed to different hosts and handle data storage between all machines in the *cluster , using a* distributed file system with multiple replicas. Distributed file systems are necessary once data becomes too large to be stored on just one machine. The system must provide data reading from the *cluster* , perform the relevant operations and write their results in a temporary environment, perform the subsequent operation and rewrite the results in the *cluster* .

It is responsible for storing data from the different stages and different levels of the architecture. The information, after being stored and analyzed in *a cluster* format , will have its results generated through the analysis stage and will then be made available through dashboards (web applications).

It is considered that the processing module has a broad scope, also acting on the ETL stage.

3.1.4 Analysis/Transformation

The "análise" step is concerned with efficiently obtaining knowledge from data, typically working with multiple data sets with different characteristics.

This step occurs since extraction, and deeper analyzes can be carried out according to user requests (using Haddop, for example). This level of architecture is responsible for performing data analysis and making the results available to an end - user level . The use of *cloud computing* in this process is recommended to allow data to be stored, accessed and used anywhere. A set of analytical procedures that can be carried out in the form of analyzes using *Data Mining* or *Predictive Analysis algorithms* [65], or analyzes carried out through *adhoc queries* [66], that is, not structured in the database.

analysis results can be stored again in so-called ready data or in a separate analysis results store . These in turn can be divided into real-time or storage results. Real - time analysis can be a synonym for flow analysis . Stream analysis refers to the analysis of streaming data . The results of data analysis can also be called a database that serves as an interface and visualization applications , such as serving OLAP (*Online Analytical Processing*) queries.

3.1.5 Preview

"visualization" stage is concerned with presenting the processed data in a format that expresses knowledge. It provides a "human interface" for this information in relation to the end user . The visualization of data involves the use and practice of appropriate statistical techniques to respond to requests that the institution will choose to request.

Some visualization techniques can generate cached information for later access, such as a report or a graph, or even include generation on demand, through an interactive interface, such as search results, for example . According to Klein et al. (2016) may include the ability to create, confirm or correct, updating data. The end user must be able to specify tasks or queries interactively in the user interface, which in turn are then mapped and taken for respective processing.

visualization tools to be implemented must also allow the user to publish reports

---

[65]Analyze a specific scenario and outline possible trends or changes.
[66]A query that cannot be determined prior to the time the query is issued.

accessible from platforms such as computers or smartphones. Analysis results are often provided to other applications. This may include technical interfaces and APIs to access data and results, and this should also be a plausible action for the visualization stage.

Given these considerations about how the proposed reference architecture should behave , it is convenient to express such functions in the format of a more detailed diagram. This assumption is represented by Figure 16:

Figure 16: Reference architecture

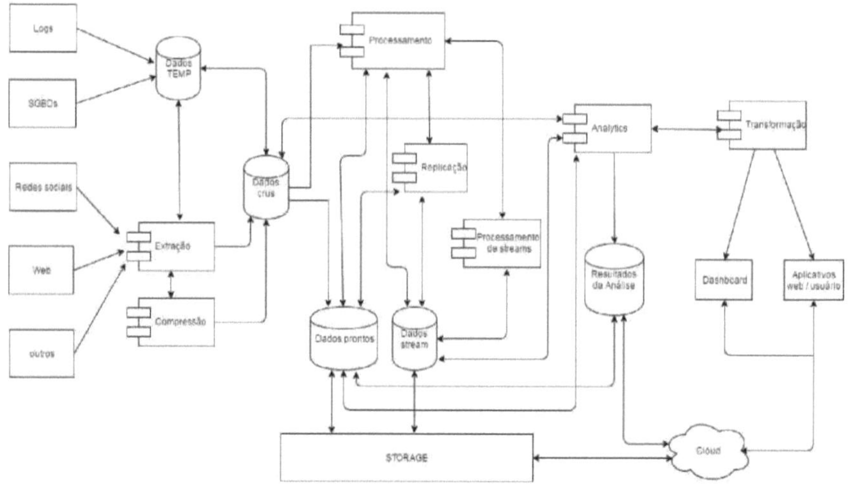

Source : Prepared by the author (2017)

3.2 Final considerations about this chapter

The set of step processes that make up this reference architecture constitutes an example of use for a generic data processing proposal. This generic architecture allows the processing of unstructured data to be addressed with future proposals for implementing a system, or even the composition of a more explicitly refined architecture for this purpose. One can imagine through it, the use of data from social networks to make decisions about the area of education , improving the choice of educational segments or even composing *insights* to improve public management within the scope of federal education institutes .

From these created conceptions , a lower level of abstraction can also be proposed, including examples of available tools on this architecture, in order to give acceptance to it, or to envisage a more functional aspect. Even though there is still a lack of greater details intrinsic to a practical implementation, the following chapter proposes an improvement alternative, through the aggregation of available tools in the form of free and/or *open source* licenses , for the Federal Institutes of Education, based on data collected from the Institute Federal Farroupilha, for this specific purpose of data processing. Finally, from this step, a way of evaluating the reference architecture is suggested , through the opinion of experts in the area.

Chapter 4

4 A PROPOSAL FOR USING ARCHITECTURE TO PROCESS UNSTRUCTURED DATA IN THE ENVIRONMENT OF FEDERAL EDUCATIONAL INSTITUTES

In this chapter, a proposal is presented and detailed in an attempt to provide a solution to the initial problem. Aiming for this success, it is necessary to first include IFFar as a representative of the other Federal Institutes of Education, Science and Technology. The requirements related to the Federal Institutes of Education are described, the prerogatives regarding the importance of preferably using technologies based on the format of *open source* licenses and finally the presentation of the elaborate architecture, as well as details of its components. Thus completing the author's proposal to build a reference model for applications that deal with unstructured data , and in accordance with the objectives initially proposed here and which guided the steps to obtain such a result.

The Federal Institute of Education, Science and Technology Farroupilha - IF Farroupilha[67] is an institution whose focus is offering professional and technological education in face-to-face and distance learning at secondary level , in addition to integrated and subsequent technical courses . With regard to higher education, IF Farroupilha offers technology, undergraduate and bachelor's degrees, seeking to verticalize teaching at the institution, observing the regional demands of each campus. As for *lato sensu* postgraduate studies , courses are offered annually that link education with the areas of training on each campus. At the stricto *sensu* level The Professional Master's Degree in Professional and Technological Education (ProfEPT) is being offered.

institutional characteristics are the legal nature of an autarchy, granting it patrimonial, financial, administrative, didactic-pedagogical and disciplinary autonomy (PDI[68] , 2014).

Before delving specifically into the choice of tools and architectures for data processing, it is worth clarifying a little more about the characterization of the data in relation to educational institutions . A brief reading about educational data, correlated with open data, is pertinent, as the processing of unstructured data may help to encourage the use of these on a larger social scale, in addition to this proposal aiming at applicability within the scope of a federal educational institution .

4.1 Educational Data

In the educational context, data of all types and formats is raw material for the development of research and studies of different levels of relevance in improving and

---

[67] Created by Law No. 11,892, of December 29, 2008, through the integration of the Federal Center for Technological Education of São Vicente do Sul, its Decentralized Unit of Júlio de Castilhos, the Federal Agrotechnical School of Alegrete, and the addition of Decentralized Education Unit of Santo Augusto, which previously belonged to the Federal Center for Technological Education of Bento Gonçalves

[68] Institutional Development Plan

technological innovation and inherent to the citizen. Important databases (content) for education, such as school censuses, are published and displayed on the Internet in formats such as pdf [69], xls [70], csv [71], doc [72] and many others. Educational data is crucial for the government and citizens, as it reflects the current reality of education. It becomes obvious, if due attention is paid to these predictions , that access, interpretation and manipulation of these data can serve as leverage in decision -making by school managers.

E-government open data can be used to assist school management through technological decision-making systems , in the design of new technological artifacts , just to mention a few examples, or in the improvement of educational resources.

However, the development of technological solutions that address this reality is still very costly, especially because educational data is predominantly in an unstructured format , which practically prevents or makes reuse unfeasible.

Furthermore, because the Federal Institutes of Education constitute part of a government in the "management" sense, it is worth mentioning that Law No. 12,527 of November 18, 2011 [72], guarantees Brazilian citizens access to public information from the Executive powers, Legislative and Judiciary, with the purpose of encouraging greater public participation, greater supervision against irregularities and through compensation, improvements in management.

Therefore, in view of the above, if institutions have the knowledge to propose means capable of processing unstructured data , they will be supporting the technological solutions mentioned above to be implemented more effectively and with less expenditure on already scarce resources , whether through own development in its entirety, or even making use of outsourced solutions in part or making up the entire solution.

4.2 Unstructured data from social networks and the importance for education

As Moraes and Gomes (2014) mention in their article, social networks have become a phenomenon of adherence and popularity, showing that countless research carried out based on existing social networks points to the revelation that 78% of people from all the ages that access the Internet (in Brazil), are users, have profiles or access some type of social network. The author also timely says:

> According to Lorenzo (2011), social networks can generate new synergies between members of an educational community, such as facilitating the sharing of information involving topics studied in the classroom, group study, the dissemination of the most diverse content information, sharing resources (documents, presentations, links, videos) and, above all, projects, in addition to strengthening the involvement of students and teachers and creating a communication channel between them and other educational institutions .

> [...] are the habitat of students, Facebook, for example, in research carried out by Tyntec (2013) showed that Brazilians use this social network on their cell phones at

---

[69] *Portable Document Format* : file format created by the company Adobe Systems so that any document can be viewed, regardless of the program that originated it.

[70] Extensible Style *Language* .

[71] *Comma-separated values* .

[72] BRAZIL. Law No. 12,537 of November 18, 2011. 2014. Available at: < http://www.planalto. gov.br/ccivil_03/_Ato2011-2014/2011/Lei/L12527.htm >. Accessed on: 12 April. 2017.

Initially, the importance of analyzing data from social networks is evident, with regard to strengthening aspects related to teaching and learning, since the data from this analysis can compel the adoption of pedagogical practices that include use of social networks, as if used in an appropriate, relevant and healthy way to the school environment, they promote collaborative learning between teachers and students.

Still with regard to school management , data collected from social networks can contribute to decision- making by managers regarding the use or not of Virtual Learning Environments (VLE), vacancies to be offered, preparation of policy plans pedagogical activities, funding incentives for research in pre-determined areas , and many other actions, given that information from social networks today forge an important tool for interaction, communication, exchange of experiences and knowledge, with regard to the socialization of the individual and your academic and professional aspirations . Werhmuller and Silveira (2012) bring to light a coherent discussion about social networks and the academic environment, reporting that, when the social network used by the student serves to share their emotions, personal desires, future prospects , these are often not are perceived by the teaching staff in the classroom. The authors also state that:

> [...] social networks as tools to support education centralize all teaching activities in an online environment together with the exchange of information from network users and fed by teachers and their students [...] Werhmuller and Silveira (2012).

These statements suggest compelling evidence to prove the managerial importance of social media data analysis .

4.3 's current situation regarding unstructured data

The educational institution , like any other, is in its daily routine, carrying out constant tasks that involve the processing and absorption of data, whether in large or small quantities, or in different formats, synthetically expressed by Figure 17.

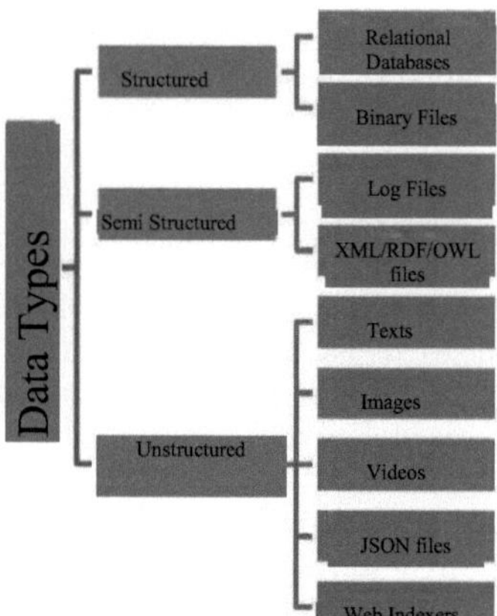

Source : Prepared by the author
(2017)

not up to the institution to abstain from the implicit requirements in the processing of this data, nor to disobey the processing steps, shown in Figure 18. According to Krishnan (2013), any system for data processing follows four stages in terms of its design : Search or Acquisition of data, Loading, Transformation and finally Extraction of results. This supports the pursuit of more transparent reasoning about institutional reality.

Figure 18: Steps of a data processing system

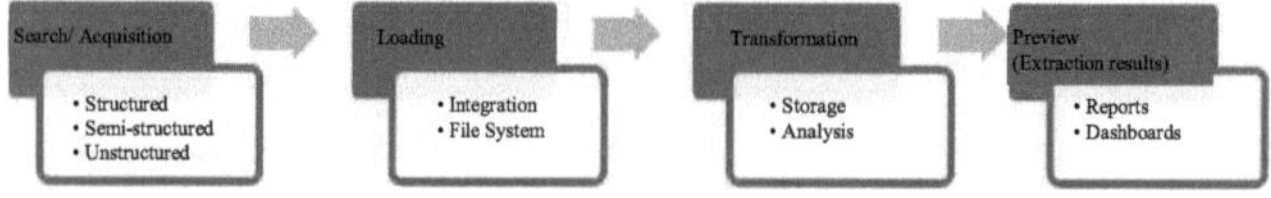

Source: Adapted from Krishnan (2013)

The interaction of institutions with data of different nature and origins, especially unstructured data (NoSQL) , as well as with the tools available on the market, some of them seen in Figure 19, especially due to the fact that companies, government bodies , among others, relates to the importance of this data in decision-making . The analysis of this data, and the consequent formation of useful information, is the prerogative of success in areas of *E Commerce* , *Business Intelligence* , *E-Government* , and many other related areas .

Figure 19: Types of data processing and tool examples

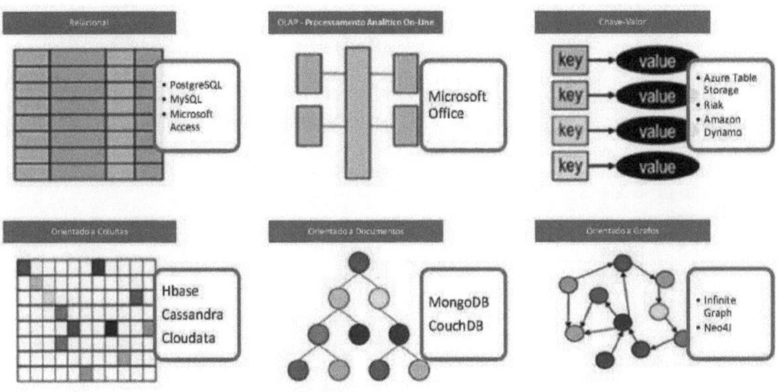

Source: Prepared by the author (2017)

It is clear that thinking about *NoSQL data* , as previously mentioned, must also be part of the daily life of institutions linked to education. In addition to the large number of people involved with the institution, whether students, teachers, technicians, partner companies, who need information to optimize their tasks and provide scientific knowledge, there is also the management aspect of processes that guide the organizational and interactive factor of the parties. .

However, the processing of large volume data in an unstructured format is still synonymous with innovation for most educational institutions .

According to data collected through the *survey* method , in which analysts and IT technicians were asked in the form of open and private questions , it is possible to measure the gap that forms between the business reality and the reality of an educational institution , for example, in that relates to the topic. Furthermore , there is clearly a lack of preparation, or to be less incisive, a lack of knowledge regarding the subject of *NoSQL* itself , and its related generators and actions capable of using it. This worrying situation is corroborated by the lack of qualified professionals, or even professionals who are merely knowledgeable about the tools that process data of this nature, in the design of *software* , applications or even projects related to institutional actions , who could use the information arising from these data to provide optimization or excellence in daily, research, expansion or management actions .

When a simplified questionnaire was applied, regarding the responsibilities of IT professionals, their training and their consequent relationship with the topic of this research, the need to deepen the topic in the institution and presumably in others remained explicit . The *survey overview* was systematized through tables.

Table 2 : Level of knowledge about the research subjects - IT Professionals/IFFar – 2016

		"I've never heard of it" / I don't know	I read to know I respect the subject	My work at the Institution is inherent to the subject
Data no Structured and/or *NoSQL Data*	n	8	7	4	1
	%	40.0%	35.0%	20.0%	5.0%
IoT	n	7	7	5	1
	%	35.0%	35.0%	25.0%	5.0%
»J^ *Big Data* Analytics	n	7	12	1	0
	%	35.0%	60.0%	5.0%	0.0%
Open Data	n	9	10	1	0
	%	45.0%	50.0%	5.0%	0.0%
Smart Governance	n	15	5	0	0
	%	75.0%	25.0%	0.0%	0.0%
Social *Big Data*	n	10	10	0	0
	%	50.0%	50.0%	0.0%	0.0%
Data Science	n	13	6	1	0
	%	65.0%	30.0%	5.0%	0.0%

Source : Prepared by the author (2017)

Table 2 proves that the majority (40%) of IT professionals at the researched institution did not even have any literary contact with the subject "unstructured data ", even though these professionals mostly hold postgraduate degrees , as shown Table 3. This number is similar to or greater than other terms that are or could be associated with unstructured data .

Table 3 : Position held x academic background - IT Professionals/IFFar - 2016

		Mid- Level IT Technician	Higher	Higher in IT	Postgraduate	Postgraduate in IT	Total
IT Analyst	1N	0	0	0	0	3	3
	1 %	0.0%	0.0%	0.0%	0.0%	100.0%	100.0%
IT Technician	1N	two	two	two		4	10
	1 %	20.0%	20.0%	20.0%	0.0%	40.0%	100.0%
Manager Administrative	1N	0	1	0	4	0	5
	1 %	0.0%	20.0%	0.0%	80.0%	0.0%	100.0%
Teacher	1N	0	0	0	two	0	two
	1 %	0.0%	0.0%	0.0%	100.0%	0.0%	100.0%

The situation exposed by Table 2 and Table 3 suggests a certain antagonism if associated with what is seen in the data in Table 4. When asked about the importance of unstructured data , especially if it comes from social networks, those responsible for information technology consider it important or relevant to the institution. For managers, the use of unstructured data from social networks is extremely important for institutional management . It is also clear that the Institution 's IT professionals are still unaware of issues concerning unstructured data .

Table 4 : Level of importance of unstructured data from social networks x Position held - IT Professionals/IFFar - 2016

	IT Analyst		IT Technician		Administrative Manager		Teacher	
	N	%	n	%	N	%	N	%
Extremely important	0	0%	1	10%	3	60%	0	0%
Could be useful in some way	1	33%	two	20%	0	0%	1	50%
Irrelevant	0	0%	two	20%	0	0%	0	0%
Relevant	two	67%	5	50%	two	40%	1	50%
Total	3	100%	10	100%	5	100%	two	100%

Source : Prepared by the author (2017)

It is also significant that all of the institution 's units still do not have any type of contact at the *software or application* level , regarding use in the institution, for the processing of unstructured data . Situation quantified by Table 5.

Table 5 : Use of *software to process* unstructured data - IT Professionals/IFFar - 2016

Unstructured data	IT Analyst		IT Technician		Administrative Manager		Teacher	
	n	%	n	%	n	%	n	%
So far I have not been in contact with any	two	67%	7	70%	4	100%	1	50%
already used it (as a user)	1	33%	two	20%	0	0%	1	50%
already participated in the software construction process	0	0%	1	10%	0	0%	0	0%
Total	3	100%	10	100%	4	100%	two	100%

Source : Prepared by the author (2017)

Furthermore, the current perspective refers to the permanence of this situation, since most of those responsible for information technology in the institution are still unaware, even if literarily, of tools such as Cassandra, HBase, Hadoop, among others, as explained in Table 6.

Table 6: Knowledge regarding specific tools - IT professionals/IFFar - 2 016

	Read about it	Used in the construction of a system
Hadoop	15%	0%
MapReduce	5%	0%
Cassandra	5%	0%
MongoDb	10%	0%
Kafka	5%	5%
Hbase	5%	5%

Source : Prepared by the author (2017)

unstructured data becomes evident and imminent , and, immediately, provide conditions so that even now, or in the very near future, this situation can be reversed. It is an intrinsic and urgent prerogative to encourage studies on the topic, directed and focused on IT professionals. This research aims and concerns this in an objective and functional way. Furthermore, it is worth bringing to the technical and functionality of professionals, the tools available on the market, when discussing unstructured data , the way in which these can serve as mechanisms for building systems and applications for use by the institution. Finally, it is necessary to formalize well-founded concepts, showing the possibility of making actions such as analysis of unstructured data a reality, inferring that the necessary investment is justified by the future production of knowledge, by making correct decisions based on information collected and processed through this medium. , and mainly, for providing technical and continuous progress in research and scientific extension, pillars that denote the accomplishment of this work.

4.4 The current situation of IFFar regarding *Data Centers* and services

The use of *clusters* It is a providential solution when the aim is to process data of large volume and variety. Investing in large, single- owned *Data Centers* is a reality applied to few institutions. However, the possibility of using surpluses in existing *Data Centers* , fragmented by institutional units, confirms that the reality of implementing methods for processing unstructured data , with the characteristics mentioned above, is a plausible act.

Inherent to these statements, with the intention of giving veracity to the above, some data was added about the *hardware contingent* of the *Data Centers* of the institution targeted by this research, through on-site visits , *with* the purpose of serving as an example and suggesting that This reality may also be present in other federal educational institutions of the same size.

It was found that, in practically every facility where a *Data Center lives* , there is, if not some excess equipment, at least a certain "slack" in the workload. This number would increase if the workload factor in relation to specific times were also measured . However, the intention is not to explain the current workload of the institution 's *Data Centers* , but rather to simply visualize the physical probability of implementing or not implementing a data processing system in *clusters* .

4.5 The advantages of using an *open source* solution for federal institutes

Numerous innovations have emerged in recent years regarding data processing, mainly data in non- relational models with exponential growth in volume, driven by the massive use of the *web* by all social segments.

free and open source *software* community in general did not refrain from participating in this evolution and several non- relational database solutions were thus created. Companies created their own solutions, even without conceiving the term *NoSQL* , which would only appear in 2009 (CHANG et al . , 2006), when the free *software community* began to develop new database options , inspired by ideas published in articles of the time.

already been demonstrated that dealing with unstructured data does not just mean encouraging efforts in programming tasks based on new search, processing and analysis paradigms, such as *MapReduce* . Furthermore, according to Krishnan (2013), a complete change must be made in the data processing requirements.

Regarding *NoSQL* databases , Leavitt (2010) reports that their growing adoption does not imply the disuse of relational databases and that each technology serves defined purposes .

The significant set of databases, already mentioned here a few times, as well as the wide range of tools for integration with these databases, already described in items 2.2.8 and 2.2.9 of this work, emphasize the importance of them being on open *source* title . However, there is still room for greater detail on some of them (Padhy et al., 2011), framed under this form of licenses, in order to allow a more detailed understanding of those that may act in the acceptance of the proposed architecture.

1 - HBase
    a) Types of data processing: Column-oriented;
    b) Uses HDFS;
    c) Uses *MapReduce* ;
    d) Makes changes to data in memory, for later storage on disk, at periodic intervals;
    e) Support for multiple *MasterNodes* , avoiding a single point of failure ;
    f) Partition and transparent distribution ;
    g) Data changes are initially stored at the end of the file, compressed periodically;
    h) To prevent failures, changes to data are also recorded in a log;
    i) Allows access through Java *Database Connectivity* (JDBC) or *Open Database Connectivity* (ODBC) to the database; It is
    j) Developed by Apache (Apache, 2016).

2 – Cassandra
    a) Types of data processing: Column-oriented;
    b) Uses HDFS;
    c) Uses *MapReduce* ;
    d) Changes to data are saved in memory and then stored on disk ;
    e) or synchronous replication , depending on the context;

f) Organization in Columns, Super Columns, Column Family and keyspaces;

g) Automatic failure detection and recovery ;

h) The same function is performed by each node belonging to the *cluster* ; It is

i) Developer: Apache (IBM.com, 2016; Apache, 2016; Datastax, 2013).

3 – CouchDB

a) Types of data processing: Document-oriented - *JavaScript Object Notation* (JSON);

b)   Uses HDFS;

c)   Uses *MapReduce* ;

d) Simple data, lists of values or other documents make up a "document". Several documents constitute a " *collection* ", which is CouchDB's storage method;

e) *Representational State Transfer* (REST) [74]interface with support for applications from different programming languages;

f) All changes made to documents are saved on disk, saved at the end of the document;

g)   Detects simultaneous updates to documents;

h)   High scalability through replication;

i) provides ACID (atomicity, consistency, isolation and durability) semantics at the document level ; It is

j)   Developer: Apache.

4 – MongoDB[75]

a) Types of data processing: Document-oriented – Binary JSON;

b) Uses *MapReduce* ;

c) High performance;

d) Documents structured into objects and stored in collections (similar to CouchDB);

e) Indexes reading and writing attributes;

f) Provides *Sharding* , in the distribution of documents across the various nodes of the *cluster* ;

g) They have indexes and dynamic queries;

h) Uses replication to ensure failure recovery ;

i) Atomicity at the attribute level and not at the document level ; It is

j) Code application , written in the C++ language.

5 - Redis (*REmote DIctionary Server*)

a) Types of data processing: Key-value;

b) The data value can assume a simple type, a list of values and others;

c) The data is stored in primary memory , for later copying to disk, when applicable;

d) Performs insertion , removal and search operations with high performance;

e) It is a TCP server with its operation based on a very simplified client-server model; It is

---

[74]style consisting of a coordinated set of architectural constraints applied to components, connectors, and data elements within a distributed hypermedia system.
[75] mongoacademico.blogspot.com

f) Creator: Salvatore Sanfilippo [76].

6 – Neo4J[77]
   a) Types of data processing: Graph;
   b) Its strong point is the speed in executing queries *;*
   c) Supports distributed transactions that involve more than one database;
   d) There is no security at the data level ;
   e) SPARQL query method ; It is
   f) Supports Java and REST API.

The Neo4J database system, like MongoDB, has a *freeware* application segment , and another version with specific licensing. It is equally pertinent to briefly explain some more characteristics regarding APIs

(REST and Java), support, database and adherence to the GPL, as expressed in Table 2:

Table 2: Summary characteristics of the databases

Basis of Data	Type	GPL	*MapReduce*	REST API	Java API	Method of Distribution
Cassandra	family of Columns	Yes	Yes	no	Yes	Hashing
CouchDB	Document	Yes	Yes	Yes	Yes	Hashing
HBase	family of Columns	Yes	Yes	Yes	Yes	Range
MongoDB	Document	Yes	Yes	Yes	Yes	Range
Neo4J	Fork	partial	No	Yes	Yes	not applicable
Redis	Key/value	Yes	No	no	Yes	Hashing

Source: Prepared by the author (2017)

4.6 An architecture proposal based on *open source* and freely licensed tools

The content of this section aims to propose a reference architecture that improves or enables implementations of large-volume unstructured data processing processes . This procedure, when associated with the intention of implementing an architectural proposal, tends to be quite expensive in terms of time and costs, given the difficulty in understanding what information is really intended to be sought with this data. However, this work aims to provide not the presentation of an exact solution, but the aggregation of knowledge about the multiple solutions that can be assembled with the tools available on the market.

Open source and free license solutions have significant importance in this context, given the cost reduction that permeates their use , compared to licensed application options .

[76] http://NoSQL-database.org
[77] http:// *NoSQL* -database.org/, https://neo4j.com

Therefore, the choice of possibilities that make up the presupposed architecture, necessarily falls, in the author's opinion, on these forms of license.

To respond to the research objectives, after analyzing the various *Big Data* and *NoSQL technologies* , the choice of Hadoop and HBase as the core of the architecture seemed to be the most plausible, firstly because they allow unstructured data , secondly because they are scalable , for They are constantly evolving, as they use *MapReduce* in data aggregation and because they are widely used by renowned companies that promote the insertion of *software* into the market to process and analyze large volumes of data.

In short, the architecture presented proposes steps, listed in Figure 20, and for each of them (which obviously interact with each other) a tooling of events about the data is suggested , from its origin to the production of information.

Figure 20: Proposed reference architecture with open source tools for IFFar - based on literature analysis

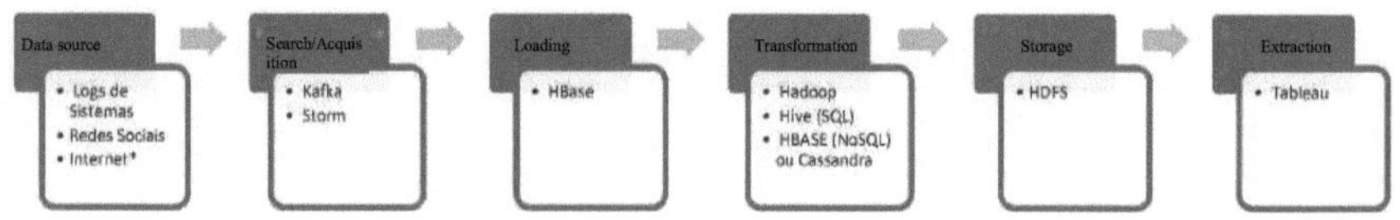

Source: Prepared by the author (2017)

Initially, in the search, acquisition and loading, data is imported from sources such as social networks, Internet searches, *log records* , among others, using tools such as Storm associated with Kafka, both free license , within what was previously proposed . Coordination of the *cluster* to execute processing tasks can be handled by Storm .

Once the search stage and subsequent data loading are complete, the processing (transformation) stage of this data begins using the techniques and functionalities that the Apache Hadoop implementation provides. The Hadoop platform with *MapReduce* provides a highly scalable and fault-tolerant infrastructure, resulting in low processing and storage costs. Using Hadoop to process ETL-related services frees up resources for downstream analytical processing .

The process of storing this generated contingent will make use of a *NoSQL* database system , which will serve as a source of consumption for analysis tasks and presentation of information to the user. Once the raw data is in the *cluster* , this database will then be modified and transformed based on the needs and requirements of the system.

Using Hadoop to process ETL jobs not only provides cost efficiencies for these low-value processes, but also frees up valuable resources to handle analytical processing . In time, the use of Hive for structured data processing as well as Pig for batch processing can also be considered.

The composition of the database is the responsibility of Hbase, comprising unstructured and partially structured data, organized into families of columns. Hbase, in turn, is an equally *open source* project written in Java, optimized for high-performance real-time queries for large amounts of data distributed in *clusters* . An HBase *cluster* is, in fact, two distinct *clusters* working together , not necessarily on the same node. The HDFS *cluster* is composed of a *namenode* (name node), acting as the *cluster* entry point and knowing *which* datanodes are (data nodes) that store any desired information . It provides a real-time, distributed database structured on top of the Hadoop file system and follows, according to Padhy et al. (2011), the following concepts:

a) tables: originate from rows and columns;
b) each column belongs to a given column family ;
c) each line is identified by its key; It is
d) a table cell is the intersection of a row and a column.

Furthermore, according to Dimiduk and Khuarana (2013), Hadoop is a platform for storing and retrieving data with random access. With this database system, it is possible to build a dynamic and flexible data model, as it does not restrict the types of data inserted into it. As HBase is part of the Hadoop project, there is a strong integration feature , as well as allowing you to easily run *MapReduce jobs* , using HBase for a data storage *background* .

Subsequently, there is an aggregation procedure and reservation of results through the *MapReduce* process that stores the indexed results in a format suitable for creating query procedures on this data.

In time, it is worth noting that the Cassandra database system was also suggested as an alternative to HBase, or even in some cases, as a supporting tool, if the administrator of the system to be implemented wants to "also" use this tool. With some very few differences, if you choose a Cassandra database, the attributes described above for HBase also apply (GREHAN, 2014).

Additionally, it is worth mentioning that a system based on HDFS includes both an interface for data storage and metadata storage and supports Linux, Mac OS and Windows operating systems.

Figure 21 graphically translates the above considerations .

Figure 21: Proposed architecture for processing unstructured data for IFFAR

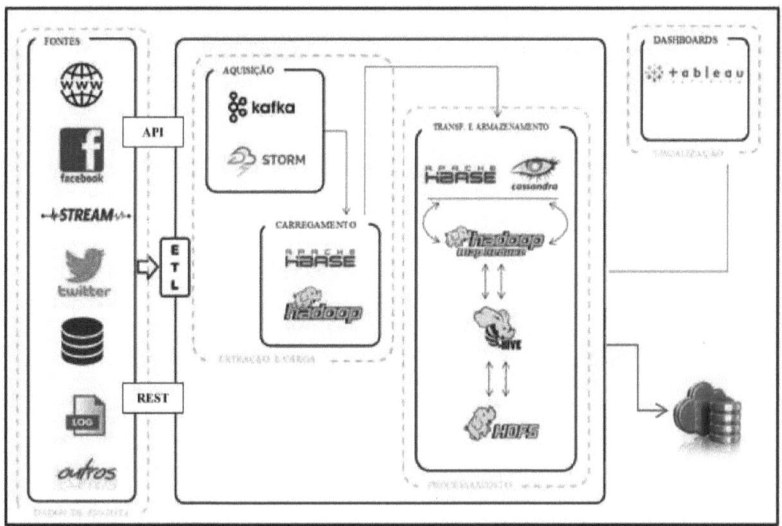

Source: Prepared by the author (2017)

Chapter 5

5 PROPOSAL EVALUATION

To better elucidate the evaluation of the proposed architecture presented, associated with the aim of understanding the role of architectural analysis within the process of developing a reference architecture for the processing of unstructured data , here is a brief contextualization of the concepts. of *software engineering* , as well as on the method called SAAM (*Software Architecture Analysis Method*), as the identification of architectural requirements for a system and construction of scenarios to define the architecture, is inherent to what this work proposes .

5.1 *Software* architecture analysis

As systems become larger and more complex, factors such as performance, robustness and quality are also considered, in addition to traditional programming techniques . Such factors are intrinsically and closely related to the architectural organization of the system (*software*) and contributed to the emergence of *Software* Engineering (Naur, 1969), whose central idea is to use engineering concepts in the production of *software systems* , given the need for deal with the exponential growth and complexity of these systems, striving for reliability. Within this perspective, a new work methodology emerges: *software* architecture , whose main steps can be seen in Figure 22.

Success in large *software* systems projects is directly associated with the premises of *software architecture* . The core context of *software architecture* is that a *software system* with a high level of abstraction can be understood and described in the form of subsystems, comprising distinct related parts, related to each other and interconnected in some way.

Figure 22: Description - system architectures

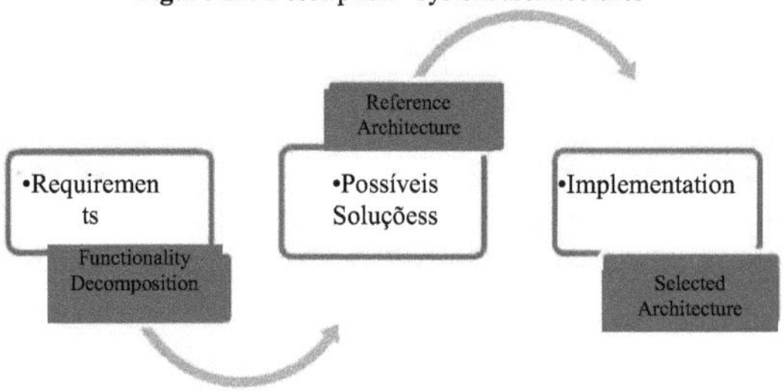

Source: Adapted from Silva Filho, AM (2006)

Not forgetting the above, it must be considered that the implementation of an architecture is partitioned in order to identify possible subsystems or functional modules . This allows a better analysis of system components in relation to their previously imposed requirements, aiming to find or present an architecture that satisfies the needs of the system itself (SILVA FILHO, 2006).

Therefore, the architectures presented will be seen as references that symbolize and describe the functionalities. This process results in providing the designer with available, described and classified architecture alternatives , thus composing reference architectures . Considering the reference architectures , it is then possible to define and formulate rules indicative of good (best) options for the design of a system. These steps are measured in Figure 23:

Figure 23: Steps in *software* architecture design

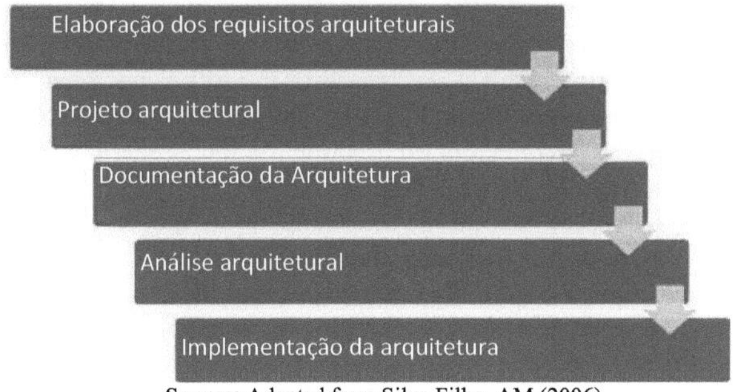

Source: Adapted from Silva Filho, AM (2006)

5.1.1 SAAM method

Here a brief consideration should be made covering the *SAAM software* architecture analysis method , even though it is not ideal for the task ahead, but with the aim of elucidating some characteristics later incorporated into the analysis process of the proposed architecture for processing *NoSQL* data .

of the *software* architecture analysis method SAAM (*Software Architecture Analysis Method*) is to assist software architects in *choosing* / comparing system architectural solution propositions . It comprises the following objectives (Kazman et al . , 1994):

a) Define a set of scenarios representing the use of the system in relation to the proposed context;
b) Use scenarios to give a functional view of the domain for which the system is proposed , associating scenarios with existing functions ; It is
c) Carry out the analysis of the proposed architectures, through the use of scenarios and functional parts, concomitantly.

For each scenario presented , through analysis , a score inherent to the architectures, objects of evaluation, is provided . The evaluator determines the weights of the scenarios considered, as well as the score of the proposed architectures.

Using scenarios proposed by the SAMM method , the analyst can use an architectural description to measure the potential of the system proposed to be built. It is important, however, to pay special attention to the context in which the system is located , as well as consider the circumstances specific to that context.

SAAM comprises a set of five interdependent steps:

a) Development of scenarios – aims to illustrate the types of activities that the system will support;
b) Architecture description – each analysis must have an architectural representation of the system;
c) Assessment of each scenario – for each scenario , a candidate architecture is determined and whether it meets the scenario 's requirements (direct support) or whether any modification is necessary (indirect support);
d) Determination of scenario interaction – an interaction between scenarios occurs when two or more scenarios require modifications of some nature; It is
e) Assessment of scenarios and interaction of scenarios - a global assessment is carried out by assigning a score to each scenario

The expected result with the SAAM method is to have, in the form of results, the production of scenarios inherent to the system, striving for quality and providing the mapping between these scenarios and the components of the proposed architecture. The analysis process to achieve this result is expressed in the following steps: Specification of system requirements, description of the architecture, extraction of scenarios, prioritization of scenarios, evaluation of the architecture in relation to the scenarios, interpretation and presentation of results (KAZMAN et al., 1994).

According to Babar et al. (2006), architectural models have an important characteristic of serving as a link between the requirements of a system and its actual implementation. The aforementioned author also states that these models are considered the first set of decisions of a project with correlation to meeting the previously proposed requirements.

Krutchen et al. (2006) opportunely state that from a practical point of view , it is possible to control the development of systems through *software architecture* . Following this reasoning, reference architectures are designated as special architectures that channel actions to arrive at the specification of a more concise and specific architecture. However, it is necessary to say that architecture evaluation methods such as SAAM, for example, cannot be directly applied to this type of architecture. This is due, according to Bass et al . (2003), to the fact that there are significant differences between concrete architectures and reference architectures. The main one is that reference architectures are generic in nature and are designed to meet functionalities of interest to all *stakeholders* in a specific domain. As a result of these characterizations, it is necessary to compose specific, or adapted, methodologies for evaluating reference architectures .

Due to the prerogatives presented regarding reference architectures, as well as the applicability of the SAAM method , the SAAM method was adapted to evaluate the proposal , in accordance with the purpose of the research.

5.2 Methodology for evaluating the proposed architecture

With the intention of gathering a critical opinion on the proposed architecture, a group of analysts, teachers and professionals from the IT, Database, *Software Architecture and related areas were invited to form concepts from a* technical perspective, so that it would be viable . show here a concept related to evaluation, even at a higher level of abstraction , synthetically expressed by Figure 24. The creation of scenarios and description of the evaluation method is described in the next items .

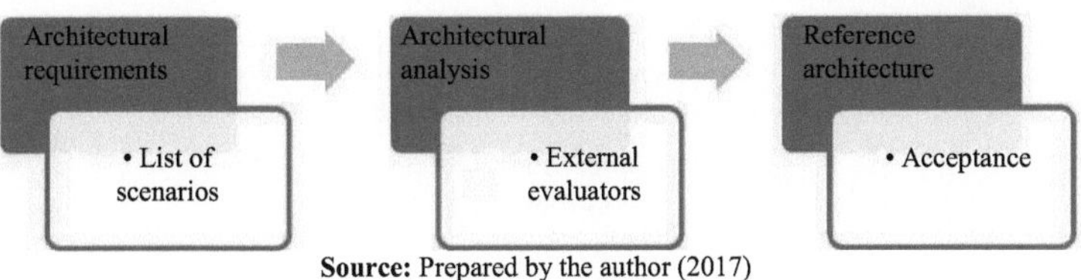

Figure 24: Architectural analysis for a reference architecture

Source: Prepared by the author (2017)

5.3 Scenarios

To carry out the evaluation process, adapted from the SAAM method , it is necessary to create scenarios . A scenario is a situation that the architecture must support and can be use cases or exploratory.

The following scenarios were created as a result of the proposition:

Scenario 1 – Allow data collection from different sources (systems, social network, databases, etc.);

Scenario 2 – Provide data loading in different formats (text, image, *logs* , files, *streaming* , etc.);

Scenario 3 – Allow large-scale storage;

Scenario 4 – Allow the analysis and transformation of data in different formats;

Scenario 5 – Allow scalability;

Scenario 6 – Provide mechanism for fault tolerance ;

Scenario 7 – Provide support for Cloud services *;* It is

Scenario 8 – Allow visualization of transformed data.

For the purpose of this work and emphasizing the proposition of a reference architecture to be analyzed using the adapted SAMM method , the author believes that the scenarios presented above are relevant and sufficient to the context, as well as the objective of the evaluation.

The SAAM method was readapted for the research context, comprising six steps described in Figure 25:

Figure 25: Steps of the adapted SAAM

Source: Prepared by the author (2017)

5.4 Description of the Assessment Process

As already mentioned, the methodology used was based on the *Software Architecture Analysis Method* (SAAM), adapting to the needs of the proposition of this study, assembling a remotely distributed team to assess the scenarios and the architecture assumed by the author. Then, as the next segment of the evaluation process , the architecture itself is presented , so that all evaluators understand it.

Next, the evaluation team must contextualize the concept of "scenario". Finally, the scenarios are analyzed regarding their interaction with each other and the viability of the architecture in relation to their contemplation , so that the effective results and opinions of the evaluation can be obtained .

already clear that the process of evaluating architecture is as important as its definition. Therefore, the participants in the aforementioned process, in the condition of evaluators, must complete the table sent (Appendix B), based on the reference architecture for processing unstructured data , from a reality perspective of IFFar (Federal Institute of Science, Technology and Education Farroupilha). Furthermore, each evaluator must have knowledge (literary at least) about the prerequisites, not necessarily all of those mentioned, but those inherent to what the scenario proposes , since some are ambiguous. Based on these initial conditions, the evaluator can then , according to his analysis, state whether or not the reference architecture meets the proposed scenario .

The evaluator will be able to provide opinions or opinions about each scenario in relation to architecture. Exemplifying adjacent or competing tools, for example, or questioning or suggesting any action, practice or situation.

The evaluator will, before starting the evaluation process, be duly guided through a summary on the subject, which must be read in advance, for a better understanding of the evaluation method and its purposes .

The table with scenarios, prerequisites, evaluation and considerations is set out in Appendix B.

5.5 Assessment Team

To make the evaluation process of this reference architecture viable , it is proposed to collect the technical assessment of external experts, judged suitable, by title or position, these being specialists, masters or doctors, to impartially assess their observations on all the inherent issues. to the purpose. The composition of the evaluation team is directly proportional to the condition of veracity of the evaluation process and despite this, there are few professionals who have the necessary knowledge to carry out such a procedure.

The evaluation team will be included in the aspects listed as shown in Table 3.

Table 3: Regarding your training/position held/ area in which you actually work

PhD Professor in BD/ *Data Mining*	two
Master Teacher in BD/ *Data Mining*	
PhD Professor in Systems Development	
Master Teacher in Systems Development	3
Professor in Related Areas	
Master Teacher in Related Areas	two
PhD IT Analyst in BD/ *Data Mining*	
Master IT Analyst in BD/ *Data Mining*	
PhD IT Analyst in Systems Development	
Master IT Analyst in Systems Development	
PhD IT Analyst in Related Areas	
Master IT Analyst in Related Areas	

Source: Prepared by the author (2017)

As for the evaluators who received an invitation to participate in the process, only one considered himself unfit to do so. In relation to the others, everyone effectively participated in all stages (initial contact, virtual meetings and response via document) of the process. Of these, 02 (two) masters in Network Educational Technologies and professor of Systems Development, 01 (one) master in Network Educational Technologies and professor of Systems Development, 01 (one) master in Applied Computing and professor of Related Areas , 01 (one) master in Computer Science and professor in Related Areas and 02 (two) doctors in Data *Mining* and professor of Database, totaling the participation of 07 (seven) professionals.

5.6 Results of the Assessment process

Each participant in the evaluation process responded to the form (Appendix B) independently. Participants were encouraged to provide comments in the form of opinions about each scenario, suggesting, agreeing,

or disagreeing about the actions or tools relevant to the process exposed in the scenario.

From there, the answers were systematized and analyzed by the author. The aspects inherent to the relevance of the scenarios and their satisfaction with the reference architecture based on *open source* tools were considered .

Of the proposed scenarios , none of them received a rejection rating, as seen in Table 4. Some were fully accepted and others were suggested some checks or warnings, without, however, downgrading them to inefficient. Below is a description of each of the scenarios and, therefore, of the proposed architecture.

Table 4: Assessment of scenarios

Scenario	1 - Answer	2 - Does not answer	3 - Respond with caveats
C1 – Allow data collection from different sources (systems, social network, databases, etc.)	6		1
C2 – Provide loading of data in different formats (text, image, logs, files, streaming, etc.);	6		1
C3 – Allow large-scale storage (*Big Data*)	6		1
C4 – Allow analysis and transformation of data in different formats	6		1
C5 – Allow scalability	6		1
C6 – Provide mechanism for fault tolerance	6		1
C7 – Provide support for Cloud services	6		1
C8 – Allow visualization of transformed data	6		1

Source: Prepared by the author (2017)

As can be seen from the visualization of Figure 26, in the opinion of the participants, through the evaluators' statements about the scenarios, the architecture proposed by the author obtained concept 1 – "meets" in 86% of evaluators, concept 3 meets partially or with reservations in the opinion of 14% of evaluators, while no evaluator questioned the viability of the architecture. Therefore, it can be considered that the architecture responded positively to the evaluation, with reservations that do not overshadow or make its applicability unfeasible. Attributes of large-scale storage, diversity, scalability, robustness and resource utilization are suggested to be covered.

Figure 26: Experts' assessment of whether the scenarios were met by the reference

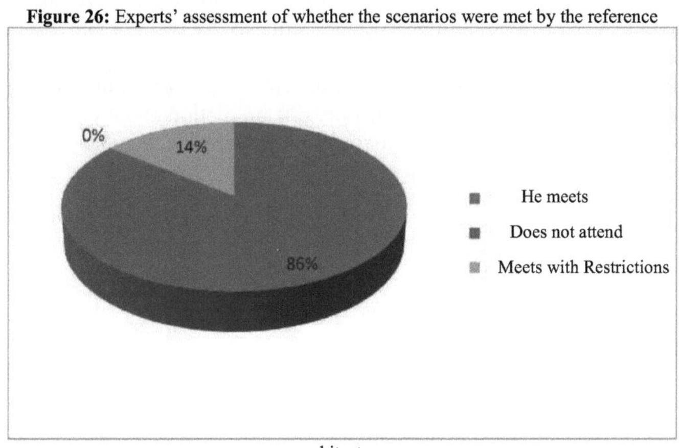

architecture
Source: Prepared by the author (2017)

Specifically, regarding scenario C1, only one of the evaluators observed that it is suitable for the proposed architecture, however, special attention must be paid to the mandatory use of a filter (*key words* [79]) to guide the collection. For scenario C2, the same evaluator measures that the computational effort to activate search engines must be observed and quantified, as well as for scenario C3. Still in relation to scenario C6, there is observance in order to consider a *Main Time to Failure rate* [80] for the so-called fault-tolerant environment.

As for the other scenarios, they were all considered adequate by all evaluators and presumed successful in terms of applicability for the proposed architecture.

5.7 Threats to the Assessment process

evaluation process of this reference architecture , previously presented and described, sought to have the effect of verification and initial acceptance , that is, it does not aim to immediately consolidate the proposal, but to bring to light its possibility or not of future use , whether as a basis implementation or just as a precursor activity to improve the definitive architecture for processing unstructured and high - volume data .

However, it is necessary to express some threats to the assessment carried out here.

---

[79] [78] Word or identifier that has a particular meaning for the programming language.

[80] " Mean period between failures": is a value assigned to a particular device or appliance to describe its reliability.

Such threats do not directly affect the final result of the assessment, but it is necessary to analyze them , aiming for future improvements.

A first indication of a threat to the reliability of the evaluation is related to the considered small number of evaluators consulted. A greater range of participants is therefore suggested in a future stage.

Another aspect, even considering and imposing prerequisites, skills and knowledge, even if only theoretical , on the evaluators, it cannot be assumed that this actually occurs with primacy, since no verification test was carried out on the evaluators regarding this presupposed knowledge. prior. It is also important to highlight here the difficulty in providing evaluators with availability to meet requests to discuss the process and the evaluation itself.

Another threat is the fact that there was no effective implementation and test cases, based on the proposed scenarios . There was only one prediction about the study of the tools and their ability to meet the requirements, based on literature analysis only.

FINAL CONSIDERATIONS

In this chapter, the conclusions that emerged throughout and after this work are presented. Since it was actually possible to suggest a reference architecture, both at a higher level of abstraction and in an aspect of plausible implementation using tools, it is worth mentioning the research work as a whole.

6.1 Work done

The research problem initially proposed questions how to treat unstructured data in an environment inherent to Federal Institutes of Education. Data from different sources such as the Internet and social networks, in addition to constituting a considerable volume .

was also concerned with questions related to which data should be processed, the origin of the data, the transformation of the data, what information should be produced, what are the main tools that could be used in this process, and of course to contextualize all this with reference to the Federal Institutes of Education. This time, it was equally concerned with referring to open data, government data, as it is a government institution .

To solve these problems, a research method , guided by DSR, was adopted to propose a *NoSQL data processing mechanism, in the form of a* reference architecture for processing unstructured data .

bibliographic review procedures , throughout this work a broad theoretical review was carried out on various topics inherent to the problem, making it possible to study and produce knowledge regarding the technologies involved with *Big Data* , *NoSQL* , *tools for processing Big Data* data and/or *NoSQL* in addition to contextualizing the importance of data for education.

To give purpose to the execution of this research, we were concerned with showing, through a *survey* , the degree of novelty of the subject " *NoSQL* " and its adjacent areas in the IF (IFFar).

This research reached the vast majority of IT technician analysts at a federal educational institution and helped to encourage the need to approach the subject, in the form of preparing this work. Details about this particular research are shown in Section 3.4.

From this previous bibliographical research procedure , foundations were formed to develop an architectural prospectus, which aims to solve the initial problem. This architecture was guided by *open source tools* , which had their use justified through technical concepts about their operation, serving as the basis for the architectural project.

Finally, an evaluation theme was then carried out and carried out (as described in chapter four) through interviews with experts capable of giving acceptance to this reference architecture. Although some reservations were pointed out, it can be said that the architecture responded positively to the evaluation.

6.2 Analysis of results

The general results were obtained from the evaluation process carried out with different experts, as illustrated in Table 6. According to the participants, in this process, this architectural sample includes the standards necessary to promote its use in a real context.

Therefore, as future work, the proposal outlined here could be implemented in a real environment by institutions that are enthusiastic about the objectives of processing and using unstructured data .

It was possible to assume that the literature analysis provided the acquisition of knowledge to design a reference architecture for processing unstructured data , using tools available on the market in *open source* and/or license-free form . It was possible, at first, to understand the dimensions that would involve an action of this size, the classification of data in terms of different forms, in addition to varied structures. Likewise, the literature analysis brought to light examples of data processing architectures used by other entities (such as Facebook or Linkedin), as well as the main characteristics of the candidate tools of choice, such as Hbase, Cassandra, MogoDB, Kafka, Tableau, among many others, to list a range of technologies, instrumentalizing the researcher in defining those that would make up the proposed architecture.

Among those mentioned, Kafka was used, as it aims to enable real-time processing of data flows, in addition to having native interaction with Storm and HDFS, and can be run as a *cluster* on one or more servers. Such processing will produce data topics from continuous streams of input.

Apache Storm can be adopted in conjunction with Kafka, as it is an *open source* , simple, real-time, distributed system that facilitates the reliable processing of unlimited data streams, compatible with any programming language . Furthermore , it is scalable, fault tolerant, guarantees that your data will be processed, easy to configure and operate.

Furthermore, Cassandra and Hbase are horizontally scalable databases that work in *clusters* , with simple configurations even when inserting new machines into the cluster or *automatic* replication of the *cluster* . It has *Map/Reduce mechanisms* and column- oriented models at its root and is capable of dealing with large volumes of data. HBase offers strong consistency at the record level , while Cassandra's documentation is more robust and educational than HBase's. It can also be seen that both are free, *open source* and under the Apache 2.0 license . The research work points out that both can form a solution for the purpose of providing the processing of unstructured data .

As for the main objective of this work, which invariably refers to the evaluation of the proposed architecture, it is concluded that it encompasses this, since the proposed scenarios , as well as the tools presented to reference a future implementation, received affirmation and agreement with the proposal of the author by experts, which had already been evidenced in the literature review , where the
Benefits cited in theory about data processing, such as data composition , were confirmed.

Still in relation to the academic contributions of the exploratory research of this work, new researchers were provided with a view on *NoSQL* data processing , in the form of an architectural proposal that can serve as an example for studies that may propose solution implementations . Also in this context, the greatest contribution of the architecture proposal was to help map *open source tools* available on the market, such as mechanisms for processing large volume and unstructured data . Furthermore , the content of this work, with data already compiled on topics such as *Big Data* and *NoSQL* , in addition to educational data, serves as a bibliographical base for readers from different areas .

The institution in question IFFar is also benefiting from the research, since the majority of its analysts and IT technicians , responsible for preparing the computational proposals to be used in IFFar, are unaware of the details of the scene involving the processing of unstructured data (as per demonstrated in the data systematization in Section

3.4). Therefore, for this, having an analysis of itself regarding the topic, allows for the addition of subsidies. The institution also benefits from proposing a product, even if it is to be implemented in the future. Finally, managers, as those responsible for a government and education, research and extension body , have in this work a vehicle for reflection and action in relation to the analysis of data from social networks, to compose raw material for decision-making.

6.3 Difficulties and Limitations

In relation to the difficulties encountered, the issue of entering a relatively new field is mentioned , with authors and works of a slightly more restricted quantity when it comes to *NoSQL* , implying that the author is constantly paying attention to more recent and pertinent publications to complement the theoretical foundation and provide a basis for the construction of the proposed architecture.

The limitations during the execution of this research occurred in the form of little interaction between the Institution 's other IT professionals and the difficulty in effectively testing, via the implementation of a *cluster* , the suggested architecture.

6.4 Future perspectives

It is suggested to implement the current proposal outlined in this work in a real environment, applying this architecture in the construction of a project to implement a system that handles unstructured data , with the aim of providing useful information about these to be applied in educational management , as well as well as making information available to the population regarding the various activities referenced and listed at a Federal Education Institution . Government investment is essential, as the object of this study is an institution of this type, in strategies to improve life as understood by the educational society and the citizen.

Furthermore, regarding future research, it would be advisable to explore techniques and technologies aimed at the security of this presumed system to be implemented based on a reference architecture , as well as tests to adapt its operation to the institutional reality. Even considering that the equipment owned by the units of an educational institution can provide a satisfactory distributed system, it is worth noting that both Hadoop and *NoSQL* databases require a significant structural implementation and configuration effort .

analytical role to be developed by the application must be validated effectively, to give useful benefit to the data worked on. An " *as a service* " model for analytical processing, *Data Mining* and visualization, in the author's premature opinion , would be pertinent.

REFERENCES

ABRAMOVA, V., BERNARDINO, J. *NoSQL* Databases. In Proceedings of the International C* Conference on Computer Science and Software Engineering - C3S2E '13. pp. 14–22. 2013. Available at: http://dl.acm.org/citation.cfm?id=2494444.2494447 .

ABRAMOVA, V., BERNARDINO, J., FURTADO, P. Experimental Evaluation of *NoSQL* Databases. International Journal of Database Management Systems, 6(3), pp.1–16. 2014.

AGRAWAL, Divyakant; DAS, Sudipto; EL ABBADI, Amr. *Big Data* and Cloud Computing: Current State and Future Opportunities. In: Proceedings of the 14th International Conference on Extending Database Technology. ACM, 2011. Available at: < http://delivery.acm.org/10.1145/1960000/1951432/p530-agrawal.pdf?ip=200.132.175.100&id=1951432&acc=ACTIVE%20SERVICE&key= 344E943C9DC262BB%2E7471D   66E3620B64D%2E4D4702B0C3E38B35%2E4D4 702B0C3E38B35&CFID=766147081&CFTOKEN=26026165&__acm__=14955606 81_5a1aaa6b153b9d6bc0ee090c0157a0a3 >. Accessed in Mar 2017.

ALVAREZ, Guilherme M.; CECI, Flávio; GONÇALVES, Alexandre L. Comparative Analysis of First and Second Generation Graph Oriented Banks–An Application in Social Analysis . III IS Innovation Meeting. Florianópolis. 2016. Available at:< http://www.lbd.dcc.ufmg.br/colecoes/eise/2016/003.pdf >. Accessed in Mar 2017

APACHE. Apache Flume: documentation. Available at: < https://flume.apache.org// >. Accessed on May 28th. 2016.

APACHE. Apache Kafka: documentation. http://kafka.apache.org/ . Accessed on: May 28, 2016.

BABBIE, E. The practice of social research. 4th edition. Belmont, Wadsworth Publ., 1986.

BAPTISTA, Cláudio. Database Chapter 2: Relational Model. Available at < http://www.dsc.ufcg.edu.br/~baptista/cursos/BDadosI/Capitulo22.pdf >. Accessed on March 10, 2017.

BAR, Jeff. Lambda architecture for Batch and Real-Time processing on AWS with Spark Streaming and Spark SQL. 2016. Available at:< https://imasters.com.br/infra/aws/arquitetura-lambda-para-processamento-batch-e-

real-time-on-aws-with-spark-streaming-and-spark-sql/?trace=1519021197&source=single> Accessed on: March 10, 2017.

BARROS, A.; CANABARRO, DR; CEPIK, MAC Beyond e -Ping: the development of an interoperability platform for e-Services in Brazil. In: BRETAS, NL; MESQUITA, C. (Ed.). Interoperability Overview. Brasília, DF: Ministry of Planning, Budget and Management, 2010. P. 137-157.

BASS, L., CLEMENTS, P., KAZMAN, R. (2003). Software Architecture in Practice.

Addison-Wesley.

BIJNENS, M. Lambda Architecture » λ lambda-architecture.net. Available at: < http://lambda-architecture.net/ >. Accessed on: 12 Dec. 2016.

CALDAS, Max Silva; SILVA, Emanoel Costa Claudino. Fundamentals and application of *Big Data* : how to treat information in a society of yottabytes. University Libraries : research, experiences and perspectives, vol. 3, no. 1, 2016. Available at: < https://seer.ufmg.br/index.php/revistarbu/article/view/1995 >

CATTELL, R. Scalable sql and *NoSQL* data stores. SIGMOD Rec., ACM, New York, NY, USA, v. 39, no. 4, p. 12–27, May 2011. ISSN 0163-5808. Available at: < http://doi.acm.org/10.1145/1978915.1978919 >. Quoted on page 51. Accessed on February 15, 2017.

CERVO, AL BERVIAN, PA Scientific methodology. 5th ed. São Paulo: Prentice Hall, 2002.

CHAUDHURI, S., DAYAL, U., NARASAYYA, V. An overview of business intelligence technology. Commun. ACM, 54 (2011), pp. 88–98

Cuzzocrea, A.,SONG, I.-y., DAVIS, KC Analytics over large-scale multidimensional data: the *Big Data* revolution! In Int'l Workshop on Data Warehousing and OLAP (DOLAP), 2011.

DATASTAX; Comparing the Hadoop Distributed File System (HDFS) with the Cassandra File System (CFS), 2013, http://www.datastax.com/wp- content/uploads/2012/09/WP-DataStax-HDFSvsCFS.pdf

DAVENPORT, TH Competing on Analytics: the new science of winning, 2007.

DAVENPORT, TH Enterprise analytics: Optimize performance, processes, and decisions through *Big Data* . Upper Saddle River, New Jersey: FT Press OperationsManagement, 2012.

DAVENPORT, T. H. (2014). How strategists use " *Big Data* " to support internal business decisions, discovery and production. Strategy and Leadership, 42(4), 45–50.

DEAN J., S. GHEMAWAT, 2004, *MapReduce* : Simplified Data Processing on Large Clusters, OSDI'04 Proceedings of the 6th conference on Symposium on Operating Systems Design & Implementation, volume 6, pp. 10-10.

DEAN, J.; GHEMAWAT, S. *MapReduce* : A flexible data processing tool. 2010. Available at: < http://doi.acm.org/10.1145/1629175.1629198 >. Accessed on: 10 Aug. 2016.

DEMCHENKO, Y., Grosso, P., De Laat, C. & Membrey, P. (2013). Addressing *Big Data* issues in scientific data infrastructure. *Collaboration Technologies ans Systems (CTS)* .

DEAN J, GHEMAWAT S. *MapReduce* : Simplified data processing on large clusters, osdi'04: Sixth symposium on operating system design and implementation, san francisco, ca, december, 2004. S Dill, R Kumar, K McCurley, S Rajagopalan, D Sivakumar, ad A Tomkins, Self-similarity in the Web, Proc VLDB. 2001;

DUMBILL, Edd. The Data Lake Dream. **Forbes: Data Driven,** USA, 14 Jan. 2014. Available at: < http://www.forbes.com/sites/edddumbill/2014/01/14/the-data-lake-dream/ >. Accessed on: 02 Sep. 2015.

DUMBILL, Edd. **Planning for *Big Data* .** Boston-USA: O'really, 2012.

FAN, Wei; BIFET, Albert. Mining *Big Data* : Current Status, and Forecast to the Future. SIGKDD Explorations, China, v. 2, no. 14, p.1-5, mar. 2012. Available at: http://www.kdd.org/sites/default/files/issues/14-2-2012-12/V14-02-01- Fan.pdf Accessed on: 15 Dec. 2014.

FERNANDES, AG **E-government: what states and municipalities are already doing** . 2000.

FERNANDES, Agnaldo Aragon; ABREU, Vladimir Ferraz de. Implementing IT Governance : from strategy to process and service management . 3rd ed. Rio de Janeiro: Brasport, 2012.

GIFFINGER, Rudolf et al . , Smart cities Ranking of European medium-sized cities. Vienna: Vienna University Of Technology, 2007. 28 p. Available at: < http://www.smartcities.eu/download/smart_cities_final_report.pdf >. Accessed on: 06 Jan. 2015.

GIL, AC How to develop research projects. 4a. ed. São Paulo: Atlas, 2002.

GREHAN, R. *Big Data* showdown: Cassandra vs. HBase. InfoWorld Magazine. [online]. San Francisco: USA. 2 Apr. 2014. Available at:< http://www.infoworld.com/article/2610656/database/big-data-showdown--cassandra- vs--hbase.html?page=4 >. Accessed on: <04 Apr. 2017>

HEVNER, AR; MARCH, ST; PARK, J.; RAM, S. Design science in information systems research. MIS Quarterly, vol. 28, no. 1, p. 75-105, 2004.

HADOOP WIKI. Available at: < https://wiki.apache.org/hadoop/ >. Accessed on 22 Feb. 2017.

KAUR, J., Kaur, H. & Kaur, K., 2013. A Review on Document Oriented and Column Oriented Databases. International Journal of Computer Trends and Technology, 4, pp.338–344. Available at: http://www.ijcttjournal.org/Volume4/issue-3/IJCTT-V4I3P128.pdf . Accessed on: Feb 15th. 2017

KAZMAN, R., Bass, L., Abowd, G., and Webb, M. (1994). SAAM: A method for analyzing the properties of software architectures. In Proc. of the 16th Int. Conf. on

KIM, G.H.; TRIMI, SA;JI-HYONG, C. *Big Data* Applications in the Government Sector. communications of the ACM, vol. 57, no. 3, 2014.

KLEIN, J.; BUGLAK, R.; BLOCKOW, D.; WUTTKE, T.; COOPER, B. A Reference

Architecture for *Big Data* Systems in the National Security Domain. 2nd International Workshop on *Big Data* Software Engineering (2016).

KRUCHTEN, PB; OBBINK, H.; SATANFORD, J. The past, present, and future for software architecture. Software, IEEE, v. 23, n.2, p. 22-30, 2006.

Kuznetsov, SD & Poskonin, a. V., 2014. *NoSQL* data management systems. Programming and Computer Software, 40(6), pp.323–332. Available at: http://link.springer.com/article/10.1134/S0361768814060152 . Accessed on 15 Feb. 17.

LACERDA, DP; DRESCH, A.; PROENÇA, A; JÚNIOR, J. Design Science Research: research method for production engineering. Management Prod., São Carlos, v. 20, no. 4, p. 741-761, 2013.

LAKSHMAN, A. and Malik, P. (2010). Cassandra: a decentralized structured storage system. SIGOPS Opera. Syst. Rev. Software Engineering, pages 81–90, Sorrento, Italy.

LIN J, DYER C. Data-intensive text processing with *MapReduce* . Synthesis Lectures on Human Language Technologies. 2010;3(1):1–177.

MAIER, M. Towards a *Big Data* reference architecture. Master's thesis Eindhoven University of Technology (October 2013).

MANYIKA, James et al . , *Big Data* : The next frontier for innovation, competition, and productivity. New York: Mckinsey Global Institute, 2011. 20 p. Available at: http://www.mckinsey.com/business-functions/digital-mckinsey/our-insights/big-data- the-next-frontier-for-innovation . Accessed on: 21 December. 2016.

MARZ, N. Warren, J. *Big Data* . Translation . 1st ed. Shelter Island, NY: Manning Publ, 2015.

MAYER-SCHÖNBERGER, Viktor; CUKIER, Kenneth. *Big Data* : A revolution that will transform how we live, work, and think. Boston: Houghton Mifflin Harcourt, 2013.

MORAES, Ana Carolina de; GOMES, Kelly Aparecida, 2015. Social Networks in Education: the importance of teacher training . VIII ABCiber National Symposium COMMUNICATION AND CULTURE IN THE ERA OF OMNIPRESENT AND OMNISCIENT MEDIA TECHNOLOGIES ESPM-SP – December 3 to 5, 2014

MCAFEE, Andrew; BRYNJOLFSSON, Erik. *Big Data* : the management revolution. Harvard Business Review, Brighton, vol. 90, no. 10, p. 61-67, oct. 2012. Available at: < https://hbr.org/2012/10/big-data-the-management-revolution# >. Accessed on: 12 September. 2017.

MAHRT, M.; SCHARKOW, M. The Value of *Big Data* in Digital Media Research. Journal of Broadcasting & Electronic Media, 57(1), 20-33, 2013.

NAUR, P., Randell, B. and Buxton, J. (Eds.), "Software Engineering: A Report on a Conference Sponsored by NATO Science Committee, NATO, 1969.

NAVATHE, S. B; ELMASRI, R. Database Systems. 6. ed. São Paulo: Pearson Addison Wesley, 2010.

OPEN KNOWLEDGE FOUNDATION. Open data handbook. [2014]. Available at: < http://opendatahandbook.org/guide/en/ >. Accessed on: 14 September. 2016.

OPEN GOV DATA. Eight principles of open government data. Available at: http://resource.org/8_principles.html . Accessed on: 05 Jan. 2017.

PADHY, Rabbi Prasad; PATRA, Manas Ranjan; SATAPATHY, Suresh Chandra. RDBMS to *NoSQL* : Reviewing Some Next-Generation Non-Relational Database's.

International Journal Of Advanced Engineering Sciences And Technologies, Vol No. 11, Issue No. 1, 015 – 030, 2011.

PALMER, B., 2010. Why not try an API? Small software innovations can be powerful branding tools. Brandweek, 1 February, Volume 51, p. 12.

PRITCHETT, Dan. Base: An acid alternative. Queue, vol. 6, no. 3, p. 48-55, 2008.

QUAN, Eilen. MINNESOTA METADATA GUIDELINES FOR DUBLIN CORE METADATA. Minnesota Department of Natural Resources. 2000.

RABBITMQ. Available at: < http://www.rabbitmq.com/ >. Accessed on: 20 Feb. 2017

ROBINSON, I., WEBBER, J. & EIFREM, E., 2013. Graph Databases First Edit. M. Loukides & N. Jepson, eds., O'Reilly Media, Inc.

ROMME, AGL Making a difference: Organization as Design. Organization Science, vol. 14, no. 5, p. 558-573, 2003. http://dx.doi.org/10.1287/orsc.14.5.558.16769 . Accessed March 7, 2017.

RUSSOM, Philip. *Big Data* Analytics, TDWI Best Practices Report. 2011.

RUSSOM, Philip. TDWI Best Practices Report - *Big Data* Analytics. 2011 by TDWI (The Data Warehousing InstituteTM).

SADALAGE, Pramod J., FOWLER, Martin. *NoSQL* distilled: a brief guide to the emerging world of polyglot persistence.Pearson Education, Inc., 2013.

SALVADOR, Valéria Farinazzo Martins et al . , Data quality for knowledge management in healthcare . In: BRAZILIAN CONGRESS OF HEALTH INFORMATION , 10., 2006, Florianópolis. Anais... . Florianópolis: Si, 2006. p. 32 -38. Available in:
<   www.researchgate.net/publication/255631635_Qualidade_de_Dados_para_Gestao_ de_conhecimento_na_Area_de_Saude > . Accessed on: 21 December. 2016.

SAMBAMURTHY, V.; SUBRAMANI, M. Special issue on information technologies and knowledge management. MIS Quarterly, v.29, pp. 193-195, 2005.

SOUSA, Paulo, 2010. The CAP theorem. Available at:

http://unrealps.wordpress.com/2010/12/28/o-teorema-cap/Accessed on: 15 Dec. 2016.

SUMBALY, R., KREPS, J., SHAH S. The " *Big Data* " Ecosystem at LinkedIn 2013 ACM SIGMOD International Conference on Management of Data, New York, New York, USA (22–27 June, 2013).

TAURION, Cezar. How to prepare for the data lake hype? **Computerworld,** São Paulo, p.1-2, 11 Dec. 2014. Available at: < http://computerworld.com.br/tecnologia/2014/12/11/como-se-preparar-para-o-hype-do-data-lake >. Accessed on: 10 September. 2015.

Tiago Cruz França, Fabrício Firmino de Faria, Fabio Medeiros Rangel, Claudio Miceli de Farias and Jonice Oliveira; **Big Social Data: Principles on Collection, Processing and Analysis of Social Data,** 2014, SBC, 1st ed. ISBN 978-85-7669-290 4

VAKKARI, P. Library and Information Science: Its Content and Scope. In: GODDEN IRENE, P. (Org.). Advances in librarianship. San Diego, 1994.

VAN AKEN, JE Management Research Based on the Paradigm of the Design Sciences: The Quest for Field-Tested and Grounded Technological Rules. Journal of Management Studies, vol. 41, no. 2, p. 219-246, 2004. http://dx.doi.org/10.1111/j.1467- 6486.2004.00430.x

WASSAN, Jyotsna Talreja. Discovering *Big Data* Modeling for Educational World. 2014. Procedia - Social and Behavioral Sciences 176 (2015) 642 – 649.

WASSERMAN, S., Faust, K. (1994), "Social Network Analysis: Methods and Applications", Cambridge University Press.

WHITE, T. Hadoop: The Definitive Guide. Third edition. Beijing: O'Reilly, 2012.

WERHMULLER, Claudia Miyuki; SILVEIRA Ismar Frango. Social Networks as Tools to Support Education , Annals of the II Seminar Hispano Brasileiro - CTS, p. 594-605, 2012.

YANG, Heechun. Total Cost of Ownership for Application Replatform by Open source SW. Procedia Computer Science, v. 91, p. 677-682, 2016. Available at:< http://www.sciencedirect.com/science/article/pii/S1877050916313631 >. Accessed on: 12 Jan 2017.

ZIKOPOULOS, PC et al . ,Understanding *Big Data* : Analytics for Enterprise-Class Hadoop and Streaming Data. McGraw-Hill, New York, 2012.

APPENDIX A - MATRIX OF ITEMS USED

Table 5 : Matrix of articles used

Article name	Year	Author	Publication
Composable architecture for rack scale *Big Data* computing	2017	Li, Chung-Sheng, et al.	Future Generation Computer Systems 67
Persisting big-data: The *NoSQL* landscape	2017	Corbellini, Alejandro, et al.	Information Systems 63
Big Data and Transparency: Using MapReduce Functions to increase the transparency *of* Public Spending	2016	Eduardo de Paiva Kate Revoredo	XII Brazilian Symposium on Information Systems, Florianópolis, SC, May 17 20, 2016
Reference Architecture for *Big Data* Systems in the National Security Domain	2016	John Klein Ross Buglak, David Blockow, Troy Wuttke, Brenton Cooper	2nd International Workshop on *Big Data* Software Engineering
An Effective *NoSQL* -Based Vector Map Tile Management Approach	2016	Wan, Lin, Zhou Huang, and Xia Peng	ISPRS International Journal of Geo-Information
Analysis of First and Second Generation Graph Oriented Banks–An Application in Social Analysis	2016	Alvarez, Guilherme M., Flávio Ceci, and Alexandre L. Gonçalves	III IS Innovation Meeting, Florianópolis, SC
Use big *data and* fast data analytics to leverage analytics as a service (AaaS)	2016	Chelliah Pethuru Raj, Skylab Vanga	IBM DeveloperWorks
Forensic investigation framework for the document store *NoSQL* DBMS: MongoDB as a case study	2016	Yoon, Jongseong, et al.	Digital Investigation 17
NoSQL Injection: Data Security on Web Vulnerability	2016	Abdalla, Hemn B., et al.	International Journal of Security andIts Applications 10.9
RDBMS, *NoSQL* , Hadoop: A Performance-Based Empirical Analysis	2016	Yassien, Amal W., and Amr F. Desouky	Proceedings of the 2nd Africa and Middle East Conference on Software Engineering
A flexible and scalable architecture for real-time ANT+ sensor data acquisition and *NoSQL* storage	2016	Mehmood, Nadeem Qaisar, Rosario Culmone, and Leonardo Mostarda	International Journal of Distributed Sensor Networks 12.5
Design Assistant for *NoSQL* Technology Selection	2015	John Klein and Ian Gorton	Proceedings of the 1st International Workshop on Future of Software Architecture Design Assistants
Big Data Design	2015	Alberto Abelló	In: Proceedings of the ACM Eighteenth International Workshop on Data Warehousing and OLAP
Apache HBase Performance Analysis and Optimization for Relational Data	2015	Neves, Francisco Nuno Teixeira	Masters dissertation

Title	Year	Author	Source
BASIS: a *Big Data Architecture* for Smart Cities	2015	Costa, Carlos Filipe Machado da Silva	Diss. University of Minho. Engineering school
Big Data design	2015	Abelló, Alberto	Proceedings of the ACM Eighteenth International Workshop on Data Warehousing and OLAP. ACM
Column-based databases: exploratory study within the scope of *NoSQL* databases	2015	Cunha, José Pedro	Diss. University of Minho. Engineering school
Connected Open Data for Education	2015	Bandeira, Judson, et al.	Information Technology in Education Update Day 4.1
Data analytics: approach to information visualization	2015	Ribeiro, Luís Rafael Araújo	Diss. University of Minho. Engineering school
Discovering *Big Data* Modeling for Educational World	2015	Jyotsna Talreja Wassan	
Maturing, Consolidation and Performance of *NoSQL* Databases-Comparative Study	2015	e Souza, Vanessa Cristina Oliveira, and Marcus Vinícius Carli dos Santos	Proceedings of the annual conference on Brazilian Symposium on Information Systems: Information Systems: A Computer Socio-Technical Perspective-Volume 1. Brazilian Computer Society
Reference Architecture and Classification of Technologies, Products and Services for *Big Data* Systems	2015	Pääkkönen, Pekka, and Daniel Pakkala	*Big Data* Research 2.4
Scalable Database Management in Cloud Computing	2015	Kaur, Pankaj Deep, and Gitanjali Sharma	rocedia Computer Science 70

Title	Year	Authors	Source
Enhancing the management of unstructured data in e learning systems using MongoDB	2015	Stevic, Milorad Pantelija, Branko Milosavljevic, and Branko Rade Perisic	Emerald Insight Program 49.1
of Research in Information Science and Technology	2014	Marcelo Peixoto Bax	XV ENANCIB (Beautiful Horizon)
Open Government: Technology Contributing to Greater Closeness between State and Society	2014	Cynthia Barberian Patricia Mello Renata Miranda	TCU Magazine 131
Social Networks in Education: the importance of teacher training	2014	Ana Carolina de Moraes Kelly Aparecida Gomes	VIII ABCiber National Symposium COMMUNICATION AND CULTURE IN THE ERA OF MEDIA TECHNOLOGIES UBIPRESENT AND OMNISCIENT ESPM-SP – December 3 to 5, 2014
Discovering *Big Data* Modeling for Educational World	2014	Jyotsna Talreja Wassan	Procedia - Social and Behavioral Sciences Volume 176, 20 February 2015, Pages 642-649
Tossing *NoSQL* –Databases out to Public Clouds	2014	Antoniadis, et al.	2014 IEEE/ACM 7th International Conference on Utility andCloud

			computing
Analysis of access strategies for large volumes of data	2014	de Oliveira, Douglas Ericson M., Cristina Boeres, and Fábio Porto	29 th SBBD {SBBD Proceedings { ISSN 2316 5170 October 6-9, 2014 { Curitiba, PR, Brazil
stores in *NoSQL* databases	2014	Pereira, Daniel José Pinto	Doctoral thesis

Big Social Data: Principles on Collection, Processing and Social Data Analysis	2014	França, Tiago Cruz, et al.	XXIX Brazilian Database Symposium –SBBD 14
Criteria for Selection of *NoSQL DBMS* : the Point of Expert View Based on Literature	2014	de Souza, Alexandre Morais, et al.	Proceedings of the 10th Brazilian Symposium on Information Systems (Londrina–PR, Brazil. 27 to 30/05/2014
BASIS - A *Big Data Architecture* for Smart Cities	2014	Carlos Filipe Machado da Silva Coast	Thesis (University of Minho – Portugal)
Big Social Data: Principles on Collection, Processing and Social Data Analysis	2014	França, Tiago Cruz, et al.	XXIX Brazilian Database Symposium –SBBD 14
Big Data Platforms : Spark, Storm and Flink	2014	Jean Luca Bez	Diss. Master's degree
Enhancing the management of unstructured data in e learning systems using MongoDB	2014	Stevic, Milorad Pantelija, Branko Milosavljevic, and Branko Rade Perisic	Program 49.1
Implementation of an open source Business Intelligence solution with Agile methodology	2014	Batista, Luís Pedro Lopes	Masters dissertation New University of Lisbon
An architecture for smart cities based on Internet of things	2014	Tomas, GustavoHenrique Rodrigues Pinto	Diss. Master's degree UFPE
DSR: Research Method for Production Engineering	2013	Daniel Lacerda Aline Dresch Adriano Proença José AV Jr	Production Management Magazine
NoSQL in Support of Big Data Analytics	2013	Joel Alexandre Luis Cavique	Science Magazine Computing, 2013, n°8
NoSQL Databases: a step to database scalability in Web environments	2013	Jaroslav Pokorny	International Journal of Web Information Systems, vol. 9, no. 1, p. 69-82, 2013.

Title	Year	Author	Source
Performance evaluation of a mongodb and hadoop platform for scientific data analysis	2013	Dede, Elif, et al.	Proceedings of the 4th ACM workshop on Scientific cloud computing.
On the necessity of model checking *NoSQL* database schemas when building saas applications	2013	Scherzinger, Stefanie, et al.	Proceedings of the 2013 International Workshop on Testing the Cloud.
Comparing the Hadoop Distributed File System (HDFS) with the Cassandra File System (CFS)	2013	datasax	White Paper BY DATASTAX CORPORATION
Addressing *Big Data* issues in scientific data infrastructure	2013	Demchenko, Yuri, et al.	Collaboration Technologies and Systems (CTS), 2013 International Conference on. IEEE
Design Science and Design Science Research as Methodological Artifacts for Production Engineering	2013	ALINE DRESCH	Diss. Master's degree
Inclusion of *MapReduce functionalities* in systems	2013	Silva, Dário Almeno Matos da	Masters dissertation

Title	Year	Author	Source
data warehousing			(University of Minho – Portugal
NoSQL in Support of Big Data Analytics	2013	Alexandre, Joel, and Luís Cavique	Science Magazine Computing, 2013, nº8
SOCIAL NETWORKS AS TOOLS TO SUPPORT EDUCATION	2013	Miyuki Werhmuller, Claudia, and Ismar Frango Silveira	Teaching Magazine Science and Mathematics 3.3
Towards a *Big Data* Reference Architecture	2013	Maier, Markus, A. Serebrenik, and ITP Vanderfeesten	Master's Thesis University of Eindhoven
Education Support Tools	2012	Claudia Miyuki Werhmuller Ismar Frango Silveira	Annals of the II Brazilian Hispano Seminar - CTS, p. 594-605, 2012
I/O Characteristics of *NoSQL* Databases	2012	Jiri Schindler	. Proceedings of the VLDB Endowment

Title	Year	Authors	Publication
NoSQL Databases : concepts, tools, languages and case studies in the context of *Big Data*	2012	Vieira, Marcos Rodrigues, et al.	Brazilian Symposium on Databases
NoSQL Databases	2012	Cardoso, Ricardo Manuel Fonseca	Diss. Superior Institute of Engineering of Porto
RDBMS to *NoSQL* : Reviewing Some Next-Generation Non-Relational Database's	2011	Rabbi Prasad Padhy Manas Ranjan Patra Suresh Chandra Satapathy	International Journal Of Advanced Engineering Sciences And Technologies, Vol No. 11, Issue No. 1, 015 - 030
NoSQL approach – a real alternative	2011	Renato Molina Toth	Sorocaba, São Paulo, Brazil: April, v. 13, 2011.
On the elasticity of *NoSQL* databases over cloud management platforms.	2011	KONSTANTINOU, Ioannis et al.	Proceedings of the 20th ACM international conference on Information and knowledge management.
Big Data and cloud computing: current state and future opportunities	2011	Agrawal, Divyakant, Sudipto Das, and Amr El Abbadi	Proceedings of the 14th International Conference on Extending Database Technology. ACM
RDBMS to *NoSQL* _Reviewing Some Next-Generation Non-Relational Database's	2011	Padhy, Rabbi Prasad, Manas Ranjan Patra, and Suresh Chandra Satapathy	International Journal of Advanced Engineering Science and Technologies
NoSQL on web 2.0: A comparative study of non-relational databases for data storage on web 2.0	2010	By Diana, Mauricio, and Marco Aurelio Gerosa	Database Thesis and Dissertation Workshop
Government : An Insight into the Importance of Theme	2009	João Batista Ferri de Oliveira	Electronic Magazine Public Informatics Year 11
A Survey of Evaluation Methods for Specific Software Architectures	2009	Lucas Bueno Ruas de Oliveira Elisa Yumi Nakagawa	3rd Brazilian Symposium on Software Components, Architectures and Reuse
Electronic Government in Brazil: Historical Perspective Starting from a Structured Analysis Model	2008	Diniz, et. Al	Administration Magazine Public
About the Importance of Software Architecture in Software Systems Development	2006	Antonio Mendes da Silva Filho	Union of Brazilian Institutes of Technology 52050-002 – Recife – PE – Brazil

APPENDIX B - SCENARIOS THAT ARCHITECTURE SHOULD MEET EVALUATOR PREREQUISITES AND OPINIONS

Scenario	Prerequisites that the evaluator must have to evaluate the architecture in relation to the scenario	Assessment 1 - He meets 2 - Does not attend 3 - He meets Partially	Seem Comments
C1 – Allow data collection from different sources (systems, social network, DBs, etc.)	Academic training with specialization in Database/ *Data Mining* / Systems Analysis Have knowledge about unstructured data / BI (*Business Intelligence*)/ETL (extraction, transformation and loading)/ *Data Warehouse* Get to know the Kafka/Storm/Talend/other Tool		
C2 – Provide loading of data in different formats (text, image, *logs* , files, *streaming* , etc.);	Academic training with specialization in Database / *Data Mining* / Data Analysis Systems/Systems Development Have knowledge about *NoSQL* /Hadoop/ *MapReduce* /ETL (extraction, transformation and load)/ *Clusters* Get to know the Haddop HDFS/Apache Hbase/Hive/Cassandra/Spark/others Tool		
C3 – Allow large-scale storage (*Big Data*)	Academic training with specialization in Database/ *Data Mining* / Systems Analysis/Systems Development Have knowledge about *Big Data* / *NoSQL* /Hadoop/ *MapReduce* /ETL (extraction,		

	transformation and load)/ *Clusters* Get to know the Haddop HDFS/Apache Hbase/Hive/Cassandra/MongoDB/CouchDB/Spark/others Tool		
C4 – Allow analysis and transformation of data in different formats	Academic training with specialization in Database/ *Data Mining* / Systems Analysis/Systems Development Have knowledge about *Big Data* / *NoSQL* /Hadoop/ *MapReduce* /ETL (extraction, transformation and load)/ Data Center/Virtualization/ *Cloud Computing* Get to know the PIG Tool/Haddop HDFS/Apache Hbase/Hive/Cassandra/Spark/others		
C5 – Allow scalability	Academic training with specialization in Database/ *Data Mining* / Systems Analysis/Systems Development Have knowledge about *Big Data* / *NoSQL* /Hadoop/ *MapReduce* /ETL (extraction, transformation and load)/ *Clusters* / *Data Center* /Virtualization/ *Cloud Computing* Get to know the PIG Tool/Haddop HDFS/Apache Hbase/Hive/Cassandra/others		
C6 – Provide mechanism for fault tolerance	Academic training with specialization in Database/ *Data Mining* / Systems Analysis/Systems Development Have knowledge about *Big Data* / *NoSQL* /Hadoop/ *MapReduce* /ETL (extraction, transformation and load)/ *Clusters* / *Data Center* /Virtualization/Cloud Computing Get to know the PIG Tool/Haddop HDFS/Apache Hbase/Hive/Cassandra/Spark/others		
C7 – Provide support for service	Academic training with specialization in Database/ *Data Mining* / Systems Analysis/Systems Development		

| *Cloud* | Have knowledge about *Big Data* / *NoSQL* /Hadoop/ *MapReduce* /ETL (extraction, transformation and load)/ *Clusters* / *Data Center* /Virtualization/ *Cloud Computing*
Get to know the PIG Tool/Haddop HDFS/Apache Hbase/Hive/Cassandra/others | | |
| C8 – Allow visualization of transformed data | Academic training with specialization in Database/ *Data Mining* / Systems Analysis/Systems Development
Have knowledge about *Big Data* / *NoSQL* /Hadoop/ *MapReduce* /ETL (extraction, transformation and load)/ *Clusters* / *Data Center* /Virtualization/ *Cloud Computing*
Get to know the PIG/Haddop HDFS/Apache Hbase/Hive/Cassandra/Tableau/Talend/Microsoft Tool Office/others | | |

Guidelines:

The evaluator must complete the table above, based on the reference architecture for processing unstructured data , from a reality perspective of IFFar (Federal Institute of Science, Technology and Education Farroupilha).

The evaluator must have knowledge (literary at least) about the prerequisites, not necessarily all of those mentioned, but those inherent to what the scenario proposes , since some are ambiguous.

The evaluator, according to his analysis, will state whether the reference architecture meets (1,2,3) the proposed scenario .

The evaluator will be able to provide opinions or opinions about each scenario in relation to architecture. Exemplifying adjacent or competing tools, for example, or questioning or suggesting any action, practice or situation.

The evaluator must read the following summary in advance, to better understand the evaluation method and its purposes .

Buy your books fast and straightforward online - at one of world's fastest growing online book stores! Environmentally sound due to Print-on-Demand technologies.

Buy your books online at
www.morebooks.shop

Kaufen Sie Ihre Bücher schnell und unkompliziert online – auf einer der am schnellsten wachsenden Buchhandelsplattformen weltweit! Dank Print-On-Demand umwelt- und ressourcenschonend produzi ert.

Bücher schneller online kaufen
www.morebooks.shop

Printed by Books on Demand GmbH, Norderstedt / Germany